MW01251937

Thanks to...

...All the authors and works in the bibliography. I admire your work and contributions to this arena.

Heath Potter, design specialist and web-master, for all your hard work in your hectic schedule.

My readers: Anne, Lisa, Nathan, Steve, et al.

Life and its funny way of telling me what I need to do next.

Introduction

Key Ideas

Business Change Today

The world has changed. It wasn't that many years ago that people stayed in one job their entire life. Companies and employees had tremendous loyalty. Businesses were stable and rooted in tradition. Your only competition was another American company, probably situated in the same city. You knew everybody in your whole division – because you had all been there awhile and because you weren't that big. And after a long time, you got a gold watch when you decided to retire.

Today employees seem to move in and out of groups and teams on almost a monthly basis. Businesses are struggling to maintain their edge because their competition may be literally half a world away. Mergers, acquisitions, down-sizing, re-structuring, new managers taking over teams, and the latest management crazes seem to come from all directions with no end in sight. There is little that is sacred anymore, much less stable. Turmoil seems to be omnipresent.

Non-Stop Change

Fundamentally human beings like stability. Even the most creative, flexible, free-spirited of us like to have things in our lives that give us a sense of belonging, balance, and safety. In many ways that sense of security has disappeared from our work lives over the past few decades.

Change, constant change, is a given in the business world today. Dealing with it is a matter of survival – not only survival for the business, but survival for the individual as well. This is something that employees and business leaders need to consider daily, because we literally do not know what the next day or week may bring.

1

How can we work and be successful in this type of environment? How do we deal with the disruptions, upset, and turmoil caused by the omnipresent flux internally and externally that impacts our ability to fundamentally do our job?

It is called Leadership

If you spend any amount of time reading the business leadership literature and/or the business change, innovation, re-structuring literature, you will find oodles of suggestions and ideas about leadership, leadership through change, dealing with mergers, acquisitions, and restructuring, and even what not to do as related to all of these.

There are lots of good ideas, suggestions, formulas, and guidelines. However, fundamentally I believe it really all boils down to leadership – good, intelligent, inspired, practical, knowledgeable leadership.

This book focuses on knowledgeable leadership: What you need to know to help you deal with change as a leader. It presumes you are already inspired, good, intelligent, and practical.

> Book II of this series of three works, *Honoring Work and Life: 99 Words for Leaders to Live By*, is about good, practical, intelligent, inspired leadership. It approaches these ideas through a discussion of values and qualities leaders should consider in their approach to managing others. The first work in this series, *Difficult Situations: Dealing with Change*, provides basic knowledge for working with and through change.

We like to think we have a handle on leading others through change. The truth is change, especially dramatic change, hits us all hard. The more you know about change, its impact, and what leadership skills you can use to make a difference, the better you and your team/group/business will be able to deal with difficulties that arise and the constant fluctuations that are more often the norm than not in the business world today.

Be a Leader

For this Introduction I chose five terms to highlight from the ninety-nine chosen for *Honoring Work and Life*: Integrity, Honesty, Ownership, Responsibility, and Caring. Though I do

2

believe it is well worthwhile to consider and reflect on all 99 terms, these leapt out at me when I began considering this book on Leadership and Change.

These terms are discussed at length in *Honoring Work and Life: 99 Words for Leaders to Live By*. Here the focus is on how they impact our leadership through change.

Integrity

Your leadership may be the single most crucial and stable thing left when a major disruption hits your team or organization. Your integrity as a leader is the most important quality and tool you have to keep the boat afloat, your group moving ahead, and your people's trust. It will be tested.

As we will discuss at some length, change impacts people. It often hits us much harder than we realize and much more than we are willing to admit. A leader who maintains his/her own self-worth and his/her own character through difficulties provides a bulwark for others against the fears and insecurities that arise.

People will expect you to have answers, provide guidance, and make a difference in spite of all that has spiraled out of control. You may be able to provide some or most of these, but you can always provide something far more important: yourself.

Your honesty and forthrightness will make all the difference in the world to someone who feels lost, someone who is upset, someone who is depressed, angry, disgruntled, disenfranchised, and/or discombobulated.

In spite of the difficulties and challenges they face, leaders need to maintain their own inner balance. That, more than anything else, can make all the difference in leading others through change.

Honesty

Integrity and Honesty are inseparable.

Are you in a position where you will be leading others through change?

Don't mince words. Don't avoid problems and concerns. Don't delay decisions or announcements, even if it means giving out bad news.

Keeping your team members apprised at every turn of what you know, what you can do, and what you understand makes a major difference in how they are able to handle change. This is particularly a key point in dealing with the constant fluctuations that are a part of every business today. People are much more likely to deal with difficulties and concerns successfully if they feel they have the best possible knowledge base and if they feel they have the power to make a difference because they do have understanding and information.

The more open and honest you can be, the more team members will perceive you to be 'integrous' or 'in integrity'*. (Betty Perkins)

* "to Act with Integrity"

> Note: My readers and I discussed this terminology at some length. "Being integrous" or "in integrity" both seem like useful additions to our language/semantics, but there are definitely sides to this argument. Personally, I like being 'in integrity,' it is active and I think it sends a message that one needs to be proactive about integrity.

Ownership

> Own your decisions.
>
> Own up to your mistakes.
>
> Own up to what is within your power to change and what you have no power to change.
>
> Own your work and your life.

Good leaders take ownership of everything they do. It is easy to blame others, the boss, the company, the customers, your competitors, the rest of the world, but it doesn't show much character and it undermines your trust with team members and others.

The wise leader takes a step back mentally and emotionally as soon as they see themselves getting defensive, worrying, complaining, and tending to blame. They get to the root of the concern and while it may be something out of their control, they move from their concern with the problem to the challenges of finding solutions instead of wallowing in 'what should be,' or 'who did what to whom.'

This type of leadership, of ownership, makes a difference because of who you are and how you approach things – because of the example you set. Team members and colleagues are much more likely to be in integrity, honest, and to own what they do if you have set the example ahead of time. Part of dealing with change, a major part, is having the right stuff from the get-go. Don't wait for something to happen.

Responsibility

Leaders not only own who they are and what they are about, they take responsibility for what they do and what their teams do. John may have dropped the ball, but you, as leader, have to pick it up, get it back into play, and pass it back to the team.

Leaders have a responsibility to themselves, to their team members, employees, and coworkers, to their organization and business, and to their families.

Responsibility is proactive. It is a positive approach to difficulties that arise. It means you don't just take things on your shoulders, but you find ways to make things happen. In times of change taking responsibility helps others see that what you and they do makes a difference. Responsibility also shows others that you care about what is happening and how it impacts all of you. That can make all the difference in the world in how successful you and your team are in dealing with change.

When you take responsibility for problems or concerns that come across your desk,

you have created the possibility of a solution.

Taking responsibility is personal empowerment!

Care (Caring)

Care about your work. Care about your outcomes, Care about how this change is impacting you and others. More than anything else, care about your people.

> Some people might have a bit of difficulty with the terminology, 'your people,' or 'my people.' I got these phrases from my dad who was the ultimate people person. It didn't mean ownership to him; it meant he cared. If Dad said, "I have to get down to the bank and get the checks signed for my people," he was focused on doing the right and best thing for the folks he interacted with at work, not just as a leader, but as a friend – as a person who cared about the people he worked with.

Every person who works for you and with whom you interact at work is a human being. Sounds too obvious to state, but it is amazing how many managers seem to forget this when they deal with others, and especially when they are facing difficulties. Whether the people you are affecting are incompetent or mediocre, or high-powered go-getters, they are all people, with feelings, thoughts, pains, and frustrations. You need to recognize these factors and differences in them and work with every one, even the difficult ones, as human beings.

If you are in a leadership position and you can't or won't care

for the people you work with and for, then **get out**.

You might be a manager, but you will never be a leader.

> Think about what my dad meant by 'his people.' What does it mean to you when you think of 'your people?' It may be the most important learning experience you have as a leader.

The other part of 'Caring' is finding ways to let the people you work with know that you care. That is what so many of the terms in *Honoring Work and Life* are all about. We let people know through our own integrity, our service, the way we honor others, what we value, and how we live our life.

Questions and Ideas for Contemplation

Take some time to think about what Leadership means to you. Leadership styles vary greatly even amongst the great leaders of industry and of the world. What matters is that they have fundamental values and qualities that make a difference to their own work and life and to the lives of others. The more we consider what we value and how we approach leadership the better we will be prepared to handle change and difficult situations as they arise.

The rest of this book focuses on more specific knowledge that can help you lead others through change. Fundamentally, however, it all comes back to leadership. Use the knowledge contained herein to help you put your leadership skills to good use.

Here is a provocative question that we will hopefully answer as we progress through this book:

> "How does a leader develop an understanding and feel for his team players when he/she inherits them from another leader?"

Chapter 1

The Impact of Change

These next two Chapters focus specifically on the impact of change in the business world. Chapter 1 discusses important general information about the impact of change. Chapter 2 focuses on specific areas leaders need to be concerned with.

It might be tempting to skip these next two chapters on the impact of change because you feel fairly confident about this topic. The reality is most of us don't fully understand how dramatic change can and does affect us; and, just as importantly in our role as a leader, how it can impact all the people around us: our employees; team members; coworkers and peers; our boss(es); our family and friends; and yes, even strangers we meet in passing.

My book, *Difficult Situations: Dealing with Change*, discusses the "Impact of change" from a broad perspective. Part II, Chapters 8 through 13, is all about the effects of change and loss. Part I, "Understanding Change," and Part III, "Growing through Change and Loss," also have a great deal of relevant information that serve as a foundation for being able to deal with personal change successfully.

Change Affects Us and 'Our People'

Change affects our mood, our stability, and our sense of well-being. When life is disruptive we react. We try to regain and then maintain our personal sense of who we are and how we fit into things. Everyone we encounter is affected by that effort to re-balance.

As a leader we are also responsible for understanding how change is affecting 'our people.' We can get so wrapped up in trying to regain our own stability that we neglect to really pay attention to how others are feeling and reacting.

Everyone is affected by Change

We may put on a brave face. We may bury our feelings and push doggedly ahead through the turmoil. We may just give in and go with the flow. We may react strongly, angrily, emotionally. We might resist or deny the effects and impact of the change. We might even avoid everything remotely concerned with what is happening and go on as if nothing has happened.

People are affected by change differently. You might be calm, cool, and collected during times of great stress, rising to the challenges that present themselves and using the tensions of the moment to fuel your efforts. One of your coworkers might be devastated by the same concerns and sink into a deep depression. Another employee may react angrily and resist everything that is happening, fueling even more turmoil in the unit. We might react with cool control in a major crisis, but be hit hard by a small change in the work structure. You cannot predict how you or someone else will react.

Leaders need to keep tabs on their own reactions and responses to the stress and challenges of change and they need to try to understand how change may be affecting their employees and compatriots. The more you know, the more likely you will be able to successfully move through the change and the problems that arise during the transition process. AND the better you will be able to assist others with their concerns as well.

Change takes Time

Even little changes, like a new employee taking over a position on a team when another member has been promoted, can cause major adjustments. These are adjustments you, individual team members, the team as a unit, and all the people that the team impacts have to make. This type of 'minor' change and many more like it are typical of the constant fluctuations in business today. It often seems that this type of restructuring is almost a constant part of your unit work-load. Each change takes time to assimilate, i.e., for us to 'get used to.' This makes staying on top of all that is transpiring even more important.

Good leaders pay attention and keep their fingers on the pulse of their teams and team members to insure that transitions are moving ahead in spite of the concerns, feelings, reactions everyone has, and adjustments everyone is making.

There are Losses and Gains

Through any change process we lose and we gain. We may gain a promotion, but lose contact with many of the employees and friends who had become so much a part of who we were and what we were about at work. At the same time we are gaining new acquaintances, we are learning new things, and we are accepting and struggling with new challenges.

Very important: Everyone we interact with in any way is also making similar adjustments. And some of the people it impacts, maybe most, if the change is unwanted (like a hostile takeover), are not happy about it.

A leader often has to lead others to the river and encourage them to wade in. It is critical that leaders show the potential gains in a change situation, as well as to be there to help employees work through the difficulties associated with the losses they face.

Own the Problem; Own the Solution

Leadership focuses on solutions to problems. When we face change, particularly major transitions that have been thrust upon us from without (outside of our control) or those significant changes that we instigate but others are resisting, we also need to get people on-board the problems that arise – in other words, they need to understand why the change is necessary. When people understand what is happening and have an understanding about the concerns or problems that have inspired the change, they can buy into the solutions to the PROBLEMS, not just the goals or potential outcomes (see Chapter 4).

Getting to goal 'A' is about leading and it is about getting people on board the 'A' train. This is fundamentally a good approach to getting teams moving toward a goal. Letting go of 'B' may be a much harder sell unless they understand why 'B' isn't working or isn't as good as 'A' is projected to be. Help them to own the problems and concerns that have generated the changes inherent in plan 'A' and you will probably have considerably less resistance and more direction through the change process.

Change is a Process

However you look at change, it takes time and we go through a great deal, a long transition process, before we emerge at the 'other end.'

> You can further consider aspects of the impact of the change process by reviewing the "Stages of Grief"/Stages of Change, (see *Difficult Situations: Dealing with Change*, Chapter 6 and 7) or by delineating transition 'phases' you feel your team will need to go through (see also Bridges, *Transitions*, "Endings, The Neutral Zone, Making A Beginning," pp. 89-150).]

From the time people become aware of the possibility of dramatic change the process has started:

> "Our company has received a takeover bid by company 'X'."

Even the announcement of a pending change affects people. People start to worry, they may be in shock, productivity may suffer, etc. Their reactions are a normal part of the change process. That process (and the many reactions to change) continues through many fluctuations until everyone on your team and within your purview feels comfortable with 'the new.' The truth is there are rarely finite beginnings (the change starts NOW!) or finite endings to the change process, (i.e. We have arrived!).

Leaders deal with the PROCESS of change – in the business world today, the process of change, one thing or another, never completely resolves.

The most important consideration for leaders is that they understand that change is not a sudden shift that everyone makes, that everyone is comfortable with, and then we all move on without looking back. All the different aspects of the impact of change that we will discuss in the next Chapter are not only possible, but likely to occur, in any significant change process.

People will be upset, depressed, angry, resistant, confused, lost, and so on. These reactions will not just happen at the beginning of the change process, but continue throughout the long transition to the 'new.'

As an example: a merger can affect employees from both

companies for many years afterward. The merging of two cultures may not be totally complete until everyone from both former cultures has retired or moved on. Hopefully, under quality leadership, the people will have learned to coexist effectively in spite of the differences in their cultures and how they 'used to do things.'

Under quality leadership the merging of diverse peoples and cultures can also have many benefits. It is often about how we end up perceiving something: that it has value and learning potential for all concerned, or that people fight the change (and each other) in the process.

You will be affected, too. And staying on top of your own reactions, emotions, well-being, and balance are very important to your being able to help lead others through what they are experiencing.

The process of change is about leadership – knowing how people are impacted and helping them through their concerns on a daily and ongoing basis. IMPACT is a strong word. It is appropriate.

Questions and Ideas for Contemplation

Take any change, large or small, that has happened recently at work and consider the impact it has had on you personally. What adjustments did you have to make? How did you feel? What did you think about? Worry about? What helped you deal with your feelings and reactions? Are there still things that aren't quite resolved/settled?

Then take the time and consider one or two employees or coworkers and consider the same things. "How did they react?" "What were their concerns?" "How are they doing?" And so on

Chapter 2

Understanding the Impact of Change

Control and Stability

We all like to feel we are in control. Traumatic change affects our sense of control and our stability within our team and organization.

> A new boss can dramatically change the whole ambience of a work unit, and very likely will. Our sense of who we are and how we fit in will be completely 'out of whack' for a period of time until we get used to who they are as a person, as a manager, and as a leader.

> An acquisition could challenge our fundamental feelings of security within an organization: "What if they bring someone in to replace me from the other group?" "What will happen if they move our division to another city?" "How are we going to squeeze ten more people into this office?" And so on.

Even small changes, like moving to a new building, can affect employees' sense of continuity and balance. They might feel like...

> "Things just don't feel right."

> "I liked the old place."

> "This new building feels too sterile."

We may even look forward to the change, but have reservations and moments of anxiety when it hits. Any disruption in the status quo can cause angst. Stress can create problems in production, relationships, and motivation.

Leadership is concerned with providing a sense of stability, self-control, and self-worth during times of change.

Self-worth

When our sense of control, our security, and our stability are shaken, our self-worth is affected. Leaders need to understand how damaging this can be. As a leader we need to consider the impact the change is having on our own self-value and we need to carefully observe the impact it is having on our team members.

Resistance, complaining, blaming, defensiveness, backstabbing, and other negatively-rooted behaviors are the result of poor self-worth and instability. Paying extra attention to 'difficult' employees during change processes is smart leadership. Paying attention and acknowledging all employees is imperative to moving as quickly and as smoothly as possible through transitions.

Resistance

We may want change. We may see the reason for change. We may be gung-ho about ultimately reaching the goals and solutions envisioned by the change. We may still resist.

As illogical as it may sometimes seem, we all like what we are used to. In counseling, the whole idea of systemic therapy is that unless you treat the system, i.e. not just the 'problem person,' but the whole family system, you are less likely to succeed at markedly changing behavior. When only a part of a system changes, the rest of the system tries very hard, albeit often unconsciously, to bring that part back into the fold. It is probably the single most important reason restructuring fails in the business world. Often the focus is on changing a small part of the system, i.e. 'the problem,' without any consideration for how the whole system actually supports, and even encourages, the part that isn't working.

If you are trying to change something or if you have change thrust upon you and you need to work it into your work style and approach, keep in mind the importance of changing the system, not just a single person or aspect of the system. Everyone affected by the change is part of the system and will react. They may take it in stride, but don't bet on it. Be open and sensitive to how people are feeling, what they are thinking, and how they may be pushing back.

Restructuring your line? Get everyone involved in the process. Otherwise you will have more resistance, more concerns, and a much more than even chance that the change will not 'take.'

Expect resistance. It is natural. You will probably, if you are willing to admit it, even resist some things yourself. The key to working with resistances is to bring everything out into the open, including the idea of resistance itself. Get people to talk about how they feel, what they are thinking about, and what, why, how, who, where, and everything else they need to talk about related to the changes being made and the change process. Get them involved. If possible get them committed to understanding the problem and concerns you are trying to alleviate and committed to the solutions and goals you are striving to reach.

Negativity

Typical negative reactions to change don't just happen at the beginning of the change process, everyone deals with them, and then they are gone. Reactions to the stress engendered by change happen in various ways and at various times to different people throughout the entire change process. Even if we know ourselves or another person very well, it is not possible to accurately predict how you or they will react to a given type of change or stressor. Every situation is different, people are different, and when change hits we may be dealing with something in our life that makes this event much harder to deal with.

Stay alert to how your people are feeling, what they are thinking, and how they are reacting. It is what really can make a difference in how you are successful in leading others through difficult change. Stay alert to your own feelings and thoughts because you can't be of much help to others if you are not dealing with your own concerns. The fact that you are paying attention to yourself and others can help get you (and them) into a proactive frame of mind and can help give you the fortitude to move through the concerns you are dealing with personally.

Common Reactions to Change

The following are common reactions and feelings associated with significant change in the workplace:

Panicked, Vulnerable, Insecure

Shocked, Confused, Disoriented

Anxious and Stressed

Upset, Irritable, Angry, Frustrated, Aggressive

Self-blame, Self-doubt, Low self-esteem

Regret, Sadness, Hurt

Depression, Emptiness, Despair

Worry, Pessimism, Paranoia

Isolation, Loneliness

Distrust, Suspicion

Feeling victimized, Disillusioned

Resentment, Betrayed

Overwhelmed

Poor motivation

Mental distress*

*See end of this chapter for an extensive list of common reactions to change

Important

Other even more severe reactions are possible: such as, self-destructive thoughts and tendencies; clinical depression or extended lowered affect; mental illness; combat mentality and severe aggressive tendencies; etc.

If you feel an employee is having serious concerns, appropriate professional help should be garnered. Many businesses have help available and it is common for organizations to provide additional assistance during major transitions. Make sure you are up to date on the services available for your team members.

Additional outside support may also be valuable, particularly if you are dealing with a major transition and very difficult issues. Trained coaches can make a major contribution in working with key personnel, especially those who are having problems coping with the change. Team building presentations, motivational seminars, and information and programs about working through change may also be appropriate.

There are many excellent independent coaches, trainers, and presenters available throughout the U.S. I personally recommend those professionals who have the flexibility to provide you with solutions that are tailored to your group and to the concerns you face, rather than 'fixed' or canned programs that have worked great for other organizations.

What can you do?

Above all else:

Be there

Be a leader

Care

Keep people informed. Let them know you are available to address concerns. Stay on top of how people feel, what they are concerned about, and what they would like to know. Be willing to ask what you can do for them.

Your presence as a stable force throughout the change process may be the single most important aspect of leadership that will help them through the difficulties and concerns that arise. When you get moving and take a proactive approach to difficulties, others will notice and get on board. It can quickly have a snowball effect and you will find that these fundamental acts of leadership can make all the difference in how effective and successful you and your team are in dealing with the changes you face.

Use your leadership skills as a mentor and as a human being. Very often this is all that is needed. Most people respond to attention, acknowledgment, caring, and support. They have much fewer concerns when they are kept informed and when they know that their manager will do everything in his/her power to go to bat for them.

The rest of this book will offer more specific suggestions building from these key ideas in regards to dealing with change. However, keeping these few key ideas in mind can make a significant difference in working through the change process and in keeping everyone motivated and productive throughout.

Key Ideas for Dealing with Change – in a Nutshell

Be a leader

      Maintain Self-Control and Stability

Care

Keep people informed

Understand that there will be resistance to change and that people will react, often negatively, to the impact of change

Everyone's Self-worth will take a hit

Questions and Ideas for Contemplation

Consider the impact of change list above in some detail. Can you imagine these reactions from employees? Try considering how your presence and concern as a leader might affect different employees' reactions to the stress of change. What specific actions might you take to help deal with some of these employee concerns and reactions?

Was getting out and about and talking with people your number one thought? It should be!

Common Reactions to Change

(from *Difficult Situations: Dealing with Change*)

Emotional effects of change

Negative affect is the most prevalent indication that change has had a significant impact on you. The following is a list of emotions/emotional reactions that are common to the change and loss process.

This list is compiled from many sources in the bibliography as well as through personal experience.

[J. Shep Jeffrey's **Coping with Workplace Change** has a list entitled "Workplace Grief Reaction Checklist." (p. 8) His list is a good basic list of emotional, mental, physical, and psychological reactions to Change and Loss.]

Panic	Self-blame
Fear	Regret
Being frightened easily	Remorse
Shock	Shame
Numbness	Hurt
Anxiety	Sadness
Stress	Emptiness
Upset	Depressed
Worry	Devastated
Anger	Despair
Irritability	Isolation
Negative affect/attitude	Lonely Feeling out-of-control
Frustrated	
Pain–emotional (and physical) Anguish	Insecurity
	Feeling weak

Distrust

Suspicious

Victimized

Feelings of Self-doubt
Disillusioned

Resentment

Betrayed

Crushed

Guilt

Confused

Uncertain

Disoriented

Feeling vulnerable

Overwhelmed

Self-protective

Psychological reactions to change and loss

Discord rises

More irritable

Combat mentality/more
Aggressive

Being unreasonable

Insecurity

Motivation falls

Denial

Shock

Avoidance

Low self-esteem

Loss of sense of security

Vulnerability

Pessimism

Paranoia

Mental distress/Mental
illness

Thoughts of self-destruction

Panic attacks

Hyperactivity

Extended lowered affect

Catatonic-like reaction

Mental reactions to change and loss

Loss of self-esteem, self worth, self-confidence

Forgetfulness

Slowed mental reactions

Being 'in a fog'

Loss of trust

Recurring thought patterns

Self-blame, guilt

Worry

Perseveration of thoughts

Physical effects of change/loss

Lack of appetite

Lack of sleep or oversleeping

Physical aches and pains

Lack of concern with personal hygiene or grooming

Weak and drained of energy

Tired

Fatigue

Health concerns/illness

Reactive losses to change/loss

Tardiness

Failure to provide for basic needs

Complaining

Blaming

Lower productivity

Miss more work

Mis-communication

Decreased loyalty

Revenge

Decreased ability to problem solve

Sabotage and violence

Drop in efficiency

Teamwork and loyalty undermined

Loss of creativity

Hostility/Conflicts

Violent behavior

Sabotage Theft

Confusing priorities

Inability to perform routine tasks

Substance abuse

Spiritual effects of change and loss

It is not within the scope of this book to comment specifically on religious and spiritual issues. However our beliefs, the foundation upon which we put our trust in life, can be rocked and even shattered by devastating loss. Bob Deits, a minister, takes a practical look at the effects of loss on spirituality in his book, *Life After Loss*. I recommend it for those who would like to consider this specific approach. There is an extensive bibliography on grief and loss at the back of his book as well. Many religions/religious leaders have works in this vein and I recommend that if you are having spiritual concerns that you seek additional information from writings relevant to your faith, and also, it will probably be helpful to contact your religious leaders for their support and advice.

Chapter 3

Making It Happen

"Bob, I just wanted to let you know that I have accepted a position with MegaCorp and will transitioning out in the next two weeks. I've recommended you for this position, but we'll need to do a search. In the meantime you are the man...."

"Helen, I know you don't want to hear this, but we are closing down this branch and moving key people over to the Main Street office in Podunkville. You will be moving into the Associate Director of Finance there. I know it is a step down, but there is a good bit more potential for growth. You need to decide who you want to move with you...."

"I'm pleased to announce we have just purchased MetroCorp and over the next six to twelve months we will be assimilating their top accounting people into our group here. John, you are going to head the transition team. You will be in Illinois most of that time, so you may want to consider getting temporary quarters there."

New boss to division managers: "I want to streamline this group over the next six months. In your packet I have included sketches for the reorganization. Get this stuff under your belt, meet with your team leaders, and let's get rolling. We'll plan strategies at our next meeting in four days...."

Bam!

And you thought you had enough going on already!

Major change hits, and hits hard. It is often unexpected, and even when we have a hint of what is to come, it still seems to take the wind out of our sails (and quite possibly our sales).

Take a brief moment and think about how you might feel and what you might spend the next few days thinking about if you were on the receiving end of one of these situations or another you can envision. Then revisit the list in the previous Chapter and identify some of the reactions you think you might have:

> Shock?
>
> Initial Panic?
>
> Feeling Vulnerable?
>
> Feeling Overwhelmed?
>
> Regret?
>
> Self-doubt?

And these are just for starters.

> How will you feel in the midst of everything?
>
> How will your people feel?
>
> How will the people feel who may lose their jobs or have to move?
>
> And so on

Yes, you may also experience some positive emotions if this change has a potential promotion attached, a raise in pay, etc. However, keep in mind that all change can be stressful, even those that seem positive from the start. Something that you may perceive as positive may have a negative impact on a coworker, e.g. you are getting the job, but your best friend and colleague, Bill, isn't. Leaders have responsibility that is far-ranging. To be effective you need to consider not only the impact changes will have on you, but also all the people who will be affected, even indirectly, as well.

Major change?

Ask yourself these questions:

> Where do you start?
>
> and
>
> How do you deal with all the concerns, emotions, reactions that you and your people face?

Gaining Momentum

There are many ways to deal with change. We can follow

formulas, plan strategies, set goals, and generally try to put some structure to the 'mess,' but the basic truth is things will happen daily, and often by the minute. There are many things that will happen that are not predictable, especially regarding the reactions and emotions people will have. Formulas, strategies, and goal setting can help, but fundamentally leaders need to accomplish two things:

get rooted, i.e. believe in themselves

and

get moving

Self-worth

However we are affected by change, whatever emotions we have, our strength as a leader goes back to who we are: our basic truths, our beliefs. If integrity and quality are two of your fundamental values, make sure that they are part of every decision you make. If your organizational ability is a strength, get organized and focus on staying organized throughout the change process because it will help ground you, and give you a foundation upon which to build. As a direct result you will also help ground others and you will be able to provide structure and security for them.

Go to your strengths and your beliefs about who you are and what you are capable of. When you do this, you are not only giving yourself a focus that helps you deal with the reactions and feelings you may have to what is happening, but you are giving others a foundation upon which they can build. That is leadership.

Be Proactive

However difficult a situation is, and there are some lulus, movement is critical. Get up, get out, get going.

You may feel shocked at what is happening. You may want to deny it. You may be experiencing a wide range of emotions, from resentment to disbelief to confusion to occasional panic. Other people affected by this situation are feeling many of those same things. These are all natural reactions and you don't want to stuff them. You want to face them, think about them, and understand what this all means to you and to the people you work with.

There is nothing wrong with reacting and feeling what is appropriate to a given situation. It is actually important to face our feelings and reactions. Where we get into trouble is if we don't move beyond our reactions and we end up wallowing in negativity.

> As an example: Shock is a common reaction to major change, especially in the first few days after the change hits home. It can feel like everything has just collapsed around us and we are boxed into a corner with no choices left. There are always choices and we can always do things. Do whatever it takes to get yourself moving in a positive direction. When you have established some momentum, you can help others get going, too.

Things you can do from the get-go:

Know yourself

Stay on top of what you are experiencing. Pay attention to how you feel, how you are reacting, and your interactions with others. This will pay off many fold as you gain more and more momentum through the change process. When things are the hardest, take a step back and see how you are feeling and what you are thinking. Then work from your strengths.

Pay attention to others

Everyone around you is going to be affected by this too. Even if the change is specifically 'yours,' i.e. you were promoted, pay attention to how this impacts others. It will affect the people you work with up, down, and across the chain, your friends, your family, everyone you come in contact with throughout the change process.

Paying attention to others, how they feel and what they are going through helps you focus outwardly and also helps you begin to think beyond, "Woe is me." The more you help others, the more you are helping yourself because you have established effort and movement. This in turn can help other team members get moving too. It will help them focus outside themselves and begin to work together as a team to face the stresses and problems as they arise.

Go through the motions

Sometimes all we need to get moving is to do something, anything positive, that makes us think, react, work, produce. Make plans, envision goals, write memos – do things. When we are in shock, when your world seems to be shifting or caving in, establishing some movement in pretty much any purposeful direction can be the catalyst for getting yourself off the ground.

Momentum starters

Put things down on paper: reactions, feelings, ideas, worries, thoughts. We all tend to perseverate about things. Writing down what we are thinking and feeling helps us organize what we are trying to deal with. It can help tremendously as we move through the change process. It can also be cathartic, releasing built up tension and emotions.

Talk to others: Make the effort to talk to the people you trust and who can commiserate with what is happening and how you feel. Get professional help from a coach, counselor, mentor. They can help tremendously when dealing with change and you can learn a great deal about mentoring/coaching your team players in the process.

Get out and about: Make an extra effort to spend time out of the office and try to avoid large periods of time alone, unless you are specifically working on a task or working on things that will help you focus (like writing your thoughts, feelings, etc.). Being alone too much of the time (for you and for other members of your team) can cause an exacerbation of emotions and reactions. Talk to people. Try to focus on what they are going through and what they need from you. Personal contact will help you and it will help them.

Get organized: Make some plans, set some short term goals, and put some things in order that you have been leaving for a rainy day. Organizing things can help take the focus away from some of the difficulties we face and can even help us begin to strategize ideas for gaining more momentum.

Help others make plans/decisions: Focusing on others' concerns fosters our own activity and can, and often does, help us get a handle on what we can accomplish and decisions we can make.

Being there for coworkers and employees can help you deal with your own issues and concerns. Helping others can be a very powerful antidote to stress.

Make decisions

Sometimes we just have to make some decisions and move ahead. As a leader we need to be able to create a vision for our team of where we are heading and how we hope to get there. Sometimes this is simply a short-term perspective that gives you and your people the impetus to get started. Longer range plans can then be developed as the situation unfolds. In the following chapters we will focus on specific things we can do as leaders to help our teams begin to deal with change.

Questions and Ideas for Contemplation

Momentum is a critical concept in dealing with change. It is something we have to consider throughout the change process and it is not unusual for leaders to have to frequently make the effort to keep things rolling. Change does not necessarily have an impetus of its own. It may initially, because of the enthusiasm you have generated, but a very common reason that restructurings don't succeed is because people get complacent and it is easier to fall back into old patterns than continue to develop the new ways of doing things.

The ideas in this chapter can be used throughout the change process to help keep things going. Paying attention to what IS happening is probably the most important skill a leader brings to the change process.

Chapter 4

Vision through Change

This Chapter is not about designing a vision. It is about developing a sense of purpose throughout the change process. While a specific vision of what the future may look like is valuable, I feel it is much more important to have something immediate and tangible that team members can focus on as they deal with the everyday stresses and problems engendered by change.

Selling the Problem

Selling the problem, i.e. getting people to buy into the reasons for change, may be specific to only certain types of change situations. It is fairly common in restructuring efforts, but may not seem relevant to a takeover or merger, at least not at the team or division level. If a manager takes over a team and plans to enervate the group, increase production, improve motivation, streamline operations, etc. his/ her task goes far beyond plans, strategies, and goals. If he/she wants to affect change, be successful, and move as quickly and smoothly as possible through the change process, he/she needs to sell the reasons behind all of these great ideas.

This is one of the most common problems that managers have in overcoming obstacles to change. They have all their ducks in a row. They have developed wonderful strategies and plans (see Chapter 14). They are ready to set things in motion and they can even give their people a cohesive and coherent picture of the future. What they don't often do, unfortunately, is get people on board as to why all these changes are necessary.

People naturally resist change. Even if the status quo isn't great and there is a lot of grumbling about how things are done, they still find security and comfort in **what is**. As wonderful as the end result of a restructuring may sound, there is a good bit of trepidation about leaving the old behind and charging into the unknown future (*Who Moved My Cheese* is a great short book that addresses this very issue. See bibliography.)

It is all about Communications

A healthy part of this book is about communications. When you want people on board your vision for change, sell the problem by letting them know:

What you are about, i.e. what is important to you and why that impacts the change.

If you feel quality is an important issue, then that needs to be addressed. Let them know and see that you live and breathe quality, specifically and in great detail. When they know how you feel and what you believe in, they will have a far greater understanding why you want the team to get to point 'B' from where they currently are at point 'A.'

What your concerns are about the status quo.

Be specific, answer questions, let them explore your understanding of things and have the opportunity to provide their own input and ideas. You may (will likely) learn a great deal about how they see the current situation, how they feel/perceive your planned changes will impact them, and gain some additional ideas that may change your own strategies and goals.

The more they can be involved in the initial phase of a change process, the better the chances of getting them on board with your ideas and plans. The more they have an opportunity to provide input and ideas of their own, the more ownership they will have of the problems and the potential solutions.

Sell the Solutions

It is important for your players to understand what the final outcomes are projected to be. Give them your vision of the best of all possible worlds but also let them contribute their ideas. Brainstorming sessions, walk-abouts ("MBWA – Management By Wandering/Walking Around," see list of Thomas Peters' works in bibliography), town-hall meetings, and the like can help get everyone involved in the goals, and as a result in the planning and strategies for achieving those goals.

An amazing amount of good information can be garnered and shared if you are willing to make this effort. Your own vision may be changed by the ideas that come from your group. Often the whole process of change will be adjusted many times in positive ways by keeping these lines of communications open.

The ultimate idea is not just to own problems and solutions, but **to own the process itself**. That is where the true momentum through change will be generated.

The Vision

In this sense you are not dealing with a specific, catchy vision statement, you are getting people to buy into a conception of quality and improvement.

What they own, what they feel they are part of,

they will put more effort into.

Ask them – frequently

Moving through change is most effective if everyone stays focused and renews their purpose regularly. The simplest way to do this is to ask them:

What is important.

What they are working toward: their strategies and goals, the team goals, the final goal. Make sure this is never left to chance, or that it is not forgotten in the melee. Keep it in the forefront.

What they are doing, right now, to move forward with current goals and strategies.

What are they going to accomplish **today**.

What they plan to do in the next day, week, month to continue ahead with the planned strategies.

What you can provide to facilitate moving ahead.

And so on.

K.I.S.

This is a more cheerful, positive (non-self-deprecatory) version of K.I.S.S.

Keep it Simple!

The more complex the vision of the future and the strategies

to get to that future,

the more difficult will be the change process.

Ideally what you envision should be based on key values: quality, ownership, persistence, etc., i.e., whatever you and they can grab onto as worthwhile goals. Everything else, including specific strategies and goals, are the means to achieving these key ideas/ideals.

Whenever possible break strategies and goals into easily and quickly achievable bites.

Nothing engenders success and movement

like success and movement.

Always come back to the most basic concepts:

What is my purpose?

What am I trying to accomplish?

Don't forget

To Acknowledge and Appreciate what they are doing.

Appropriate Recognition and Rewards

Celebrations and Ceremonies for milestones that are achieved

To say 'Thank You.'

Don't forget these throughout all the difficult situations you and your team deal with on a day-to-day basis. Often it is the small things that make all the difference...most often.

Questions and Ideas for Contemplation

Dealing with Major Change?

Start by creating a personal vision of your own future. Base it in your most fundamental values and qualities. Then you can begin to work on the specifics of your vision for the team, the transition, the strategies and goals.

A question to always ask yourself (and it doesn't hurt to ask it of your team players) is

> How does this change process and my goals reflect what I fundamentally believe in?

Or you could phrase it in other ways, for example:

> This action/goal/strategy supports my fundamental value/ belief in... (quality, responsibility, etc.)

Chapter 5

No Guts; No Glory

It takes courage to lead

It takes real courage to lead and to care

Sometimes we have to make tough decisions for ourselves and for others. Sometimes we have to just cut through the crap and move ahead. It may be difficult. People may get hurt, but more than likely they will get hurt a lot more if you delay or hide your decisions, or push them off on someone else.

Through my experiences as a coach, mentor, and keen observation of the corporate world, I have seen otherwise competent managers and quality leaders brought to a standstill because they were afraid to rock the boat, be decisive, or to make sure their strategies and goals were heard and seriously considered by their higher ups.

Excuses don't cut it

If you are a new manager of a department and you feel there are a great many things that need changing, you have to be willing to make the effort and have the courage to bring your truths into the open. That means vision, planning, strategizing, goal-setting AND getting people on board all of these from the get-go.

More than anything else it means being willing to sell what you believe in to others. If you hesitate much at all, all may be lost.

Sell it to your team – sell your values, the qualities you expect from yourself and others; and sell the plan to get your team to the point where everyone is fulfilling what those values and qualities mean to your work and your team's work

Make sure you talk and walk those values, qualities, strategies, and goals. Memos, meetings, and agenda items don't hack it. You have to **be**, in everything you do and in every interaction you have, what you are striving for. **Then** others will take it seriously.

Passion for what you are striving for rarely hurts. Show others through your intensity, responsibility, commitment, visibility, character, energy, and persistence. (See Chapters, 95, 6, 10, 40, 46, 70, and 58 respectively in *Honoring Work and Life: 99 Words for Leaders to Live By*)

Sell it to your peers and coworkers – sell everything listed above to those in the chain that impact your group. Let them know what you hold important, where you are headed, and how you plan to get there. Let them know how this may impact them.

Sell it to your boss/higher ups – Most bosses will listen to quality ideas driven by commitment and passion. If they won't, make them listen BECAUSE this is your life and your work and if you are frustrated because you can't do it the way you want to, you have only two choices: change something, or go somewhere else where you can change things and be yourself. This is where the guts comes in – sometimes you just have to take a chance and let your boss know what you believe in and what you feel you have to do.

> Do it intelligently.
>
> Make sure all your ducks are in a row ahead of time.
>
> Be willing to compromise, but only if it doesn't water down what you feel is most important, i.e. the values and qualities that are at the root of your reasons for wanting to change things
>
> Be willing and able to express what you are passionate about. Make sure your plan, strategies, and goals reflect your commitment to excellence and your most fundamental values and qualities.

Do it!

Are you willing to take chances?

> For yourself?
>
> For your team?

Ultimately you have to decide what is best for you and your team within the framework of where you work and who you work for.

However, you always want to make sure you, "Choose Wisely." (Bywords of difficultpeople.org)

Your best bet is to strategize, carefully lay plans, and get your superiors and team involved if at all feasible. There are almost always intelligent ways to deal with roadblocks and resistance. Use your intelligence and ingenuity.

Taking chances doesn't mean making poor choices

Consider all the ramifications of what you want to do and how they will impact your people, coworkers and peers in other lines and other matrix teams, your immediate supervisor and those further up the chain, etc. Taking chances wisely means thinking a strategy all the way through and making sure your ideas are rooted in your beliefs and passions.

Always consider the individual people you will impact. I typically took many creative risks in my work, but I always had a good feel for the people I would impact. You can get away with an amazing amount of stuff if you keep the people, potential effects, and strategies in mind and whenever possible 'in the loop'. Pay attention to who they are, what they value, and what you think you can make happen without stepping on toes!

Courage makes a Difference

Instigating change, restructuring your team or area, is one way in which leaders demonstrate considerable courage. It also takes courage to deal with change that comes from 'without': mergers and acquisitions; restructuring forced on your team from above; loss or gains of personnel; changes in work related issues, i.e. productivity, finances; etc. These are all areas in which managers have to make decisions and accept responsibility for actions that affect many people.

WHAT you do and HOW you do it can make all the difference in how you and your team members deal with change. Being willing to make decisions and to push ahead with ideas and ideals does separate the proactive from the inactive.

Make a Difference

You do it by being open and honest and forthright with decisions.

You do it by standing up for yourself and others.

You do it by considering others.

You do it by being committed to your values, beliefs, ideas, and ideals.

You do it by caring.

Questions and Ideas for Contemplation

Change can be very frightening, for our team members and for ourselves. Admitting our own feelings, misgivings, fears, and concerns is a very important part of moving beyond our reactions and feelings of instability, to being in control. Leaders rise to the occasion by being able to get past their own fears through their commitment and beliefs.

Courage is one of those traits that is difficult to describe and seemingly impossible to teach. Courage comes from within and when we are hit hard by circumstances it may be the small bites of bravery that get us going and help get others going. You don't have to charge up over the hill into a hail of gunfire. You do have to get moving, take some chances, make decisions, and stand up for yourself, your beliefs, and for your team members.

We all have the potential to be courageous.

How do you manifest courage in your daily work life?

How do you deal with things when the going gets tough?

Chapter 6

Dealing with Bureaucracy and B.S.

Getting Started Isn't Always Easy

You are motivated. You have got your ducks in a row. You are on top of your feelings and reactions and you are making every effort to take care of your team members. You come slamming into the wall of "That is not how we do things around here."

Unfortunately this is far too common a scenario when trying to instigate change or to restructure a team/division/organization.

It is resistance – resistance on a more global scale.

What are the possibilities?

> "I'm in command now, and I'll do as I damned well please." (Quote from an old novel about a cavalry troop. Something I read many years ago; far too long ago to have any idea of the source.)

Dealing with bureaucracy and the 'stick-to-it-tive-ness' of organizational culture or the underlying culture of a business* takes guts. It also takes intelligence and judiciousness whenever feasible, but in the final analysis <u>it often comes down to whether what you want and believe in is worth going after</u>.

*'Underlying culture,' as I use it here, means a culture that is unspoken and unwritten, but permeates a team, group, or organization. It is what is accepted and done because that is the way it is or the way it has been.

Remember, **people don't like to change**.

The possibilities of dealing successfully with bureaucratic roadblocks include many of the ideas and tools talked about up to this point in this book. When you run into bureaucracy and old 'habits' or business practices that don't really make much sense but are there, then:

Talk to people; listen to people; know their concerns thoroughly and get as much of a handle on the problems and the blocks they are facing or are creating as you can.

> Make hard choices
>
> Make them NOW!
>
> Get people on board
>
> Get them involved
>
> Most importantly: listen to their ideas:
>
>> HINT: it may be the only way you will be able to get them to really listen to your ideas.
>
> When you have the ball rolling, be sure you keep it rolling.

Get your ducks in a row

If you are facing a bureaucratic roadblock, then you need to know as much as possible prior to breaking down any barriers, making end runs, or jumping over hurdles before you know what is on the other side. Obstacles that we run into in instigating and dealing with change can be the stubborn opinion of a colleague or boss, a policy, an accepted practice or a rule, a 'recommendation' from a higher up, dictates from Human Resources or other management divisions (legal, financial/budgetary), etc. Some of these are inviolate because they relate to Federal or State Law, some may be fairly set in cement because they deal with legal precedents and issues related to your business, or some may be just part of the way things have been or the way someone wants them.

Know what and who you are dealing with. The more you know the better choices you can make and the more innovative you can be in seeking solutions. There are even ways to deal with laws and policies that appear, at first glance, to be inviolate. But you often won't know unless you garner all the information available.

Yes, sometimes you really will run into a brick wall, but those instances are very rare. Your knowledge and creativity can open up many doors.

Get people on board

We have already discussed the importance of selling the problem and selling solutions. Both of these are important to getting people on board the changes you want to make, but you often need to go beyond that. People invest in something because they have ownership of it – because it is not just your problem and your solution, but because it becomes their concern and because they want the change, too.

ASK!

The best way to really get people involved and on board is to ask them:

> What things are getting in your way?
>
> What changes will make your job easier and more enjoyable?
>
> What obstacles to your personal success can we try to deal with/remove?
>
> What obstacles to the team's success can we try to deal with/remove?
>
> How can we succeed in dealing with this obstacle?
>
>> HINT: Sometimes the best ideas for success when dealing with bureaucratic nonsense come from the least likely sources.
>
> What frustrations can we remove that will make this change process easier?
>
> And so on.

One of the BEST ways is to wrap some of their concerns and priorities into your agenda for change. Then everyone is invested in the results.

Leaders often have great ideas, great solutions, terrific strategies, and motivation out the wazoo. They have no problem making decisions and they talk, walk, and breathe their enthusiasm. What they don't do is ASK.

> AND, when you do ask, make sure you listen very carefully to the answers.

We all hate bureaucracy.

But we get used to it and when someone says such and such has to change, far too often we find shelter in what we know, what is comfortable. We really don't want to change. When we are asked about the things that get in our way, or the things that are obstructing the path to our success, we are more likely to become vested in finding ways to get past the problems that concern all of us.

A major amount of bureaucratic nonsense can be solved by getting people on board the task of dealing with it. The rest of the time, you as a leader, need to take responsibility for making a difference.

Make a determined effort to get people on board, then,

Be willing to make hard choices, make changes, and go up against the 'norm' or the way it has always been done. Decide what is most important: 1) staying where your team is currently at and not making the changes you want to make; 2) finding a less than satisfactory compromise to the concern; 3) finding a mostly satisfactory compromise; 4) or going ahead with your plans and ideas.

None of these decisions are necessarily easy and none are 'right.' It all depends on the circumstances. However, from long personal experience, if I really believed in something that I felt was best for my team I went for it, either by following point 3 or point 4 above. I never met a bureaucratic obstacle that I wasn't willing to tackle determinedly and most of them I managed to find a way around without stepping on any toes.

Do it Now!

Once you have thought it out, solicited the best advice possible, shared ideas and thoughts with team members, brought everything together into an organized format, and worked through foreseeable obstacles – go for it. Whatever you choose to do, don't delay. There is always a point at which further consideration, worry, and data gathering becomes counterproductive. Good leaders know when they reach that point. They need to know when to act and they need to be willing to act.

Keep the ball rolling

If you have made your choice, taken a dive off the deep end of the pool, gotten people involved, and you actually have somehow managed to get around this particular problem, that is only part of the battle. Make sure that everyone stays on track and that this concern or other related concerns don't creep into the picture as you move further through the change process. Until your strategies and goals are ingrained into the new culture and work ethic of your team players, you have to stay on top of what is happening.

Always remember that open communication is your best tool for moving ahead through change.

Questions and Ideas for Contemplation

Try thinking of an obstacle you have been frustrated with at work. What techniques have you used to get past this concern? What could you try that you haven't tried yet?

> Are your people involved and vested?
>
> Is your boss (and his/her boss) involved and vested?
>
> Have you asked them? About their concerns, ideas, input?
>
> Have you done your research and garnered all the information you can?
>
> What/who has created an obstacle?
>
> What else can you do to deal with this successfully?

Far too often the answer we seek rests in what we haven't done yet. Very often there are more things we can do.

Chapter 7

The Process of Change

"Don't push it. Experts say most kids can't be toilet trained until they are twenty months old and can't tie their shoes before they are four years old. Be patient or your frustrations may set back the whole process." (From a "Dad's Daily Calendar," Andrews McMeel Publishing)

This is an amusing little idea that, if you have had kids, probably makes a good bit of sense.

Think about this in relationship to any major change in work (and life). It does take time to adjust and sometimes we are just not quite ready. If you lead a group of people and you are going through restructuring, or you just took over a group and you want to make some changes, give them time. Most of your people will eventually get what you are trying to accomplish and get on board your 'A' train. Just keep in mind that they, and you, are adjusting to each other.

Yes, there are ways to facilitate the process, and that is part of what leadership and this book are about. But there is a fine line between motivating people and pushing people too hard.

The best way to keep things moving through the change process is to keep the aims and goals as part of yours and your team's daily agenda. In other words, help everyone move ahead by talking about it, living it, paying attention to it, listening, and facilitating.

Look on the bright side, by the time everyone is on board you will all be adjusting to something else and the old adjustment will now be "how we do things around here."

Same ol', Same ol

This chapter and those that follow will highlight ideas that can help you **facilitate the change process**. As a leader we don't necessarily want everything to happen in its own good time, we want to help people and our team move ahead. In a sense there isn't anything new here. It is simply good ideas applied to moving through the difficulties and stresses of change.

Focus (see 'Focus,' Chapter 66, **Honoring Work and Life**)

When you have gotten past the initial reactions, emotions, and adjustments to whatever you are facing, you and your team members will settle in to the process of assimilating the change into your daily work life and schedule. Whether you are dealing with planned restructuring, new personnel, a major merger, or some other significant change at work, you need to consider the time it takes for changes to become rooted, to grow, and to blossom.

Our tendency as human beings is to make a great effort at the start of things, get everyone on board and rolling along, and then to let things take care of themselves because as a manager we have far too many other things to deal with.

Change often fails or becomes a major thorn in the side of an organization because we don't pay attention to all the little things that happen after the initial thrust. People don't just change. They don't accept the new way of doing things and march happily along into the future. Resistances continue, people continue to be impacted by the change, and emotions and reactions don't just go away. We don't give up the past so easily and sometimes it is very hard to really make the changes we want 'stick.' The tendency is for things and people to slowly slide back into the habits of old. This is where leadership can play a major role in making sure the process of change continually moves ahead and stays a part of everyone's conscious endeavors.

For example:

> We may want to get our new time management agenda off to a great start, but then the extra meetings start creeping back, the times for meetings start getting longer, people overrun their agendas, extraneous memos pile up, etc.

Focus as applied to the change process means that as a leader you need to be the catalyst that helps keep the change agenda rolling. Reminders are not once a week or once a month 'meetings' to check up on how things are going; they are every day – living the change by talking to people, sending memos, and renewing emphasis on key points through what you are doing and what you are focusing on.

Visibility

Your visibility, i.e. what you are showing through what you focus on, makes a difference. Always keep in mind that successful leadership through change is all about making a difference.

Make a difference

Remind everyone of what is important by taking every opportunity (daily) to check on and talk about what should be happening.

Ask! People figure out very quickly what is important when you ask about it.

Start and end meetings, conversations, memos, chance encounters with statements and questions about the change and what is happening: "Glad we had this chat, Steve. Don't forget I want an update tomorrow on how that transition is going," or "Are you on top of the new organization of Alice's team? How do you feel everyone is adjusting? Any concerns?"

Get out there and find out what is or isn't happening. Whatever level or rank you are, you need to spend time out on the floor interacting with the players.

Be specific. General questions are good, but real knowledge comes from occasional probing. Even if you are a fairly high level executive, getting out and about will tell you a great deal about how things are going and whether the ship is still chugging along or dead in the water.

Don't let your responsibility and effort slide away from what needs to happen to keep things rolling. If you take your focus off of the ball, so will everyone else. Whatever else in on your plate, make room for keeping on top of the change process.

Review your plans, strategies, goals, and most importantly how people are handling things. After the initial shock to change, people's reactions often go underground. This doesn't necessarily mean they are dealing with things well just because you don't 'see' any obvious concerns. Great leaders keep their fingers on the pulse of the feelings and thoughts of their players. One of the most devastating impacts to a continuing positive transition process is an employee who undermines individual and team spirit through negativity, backstabbing, and constant complaining and blaming. You can't know unless you pay attention.

Present an in-control, positive demeanor in spite of the stresses and concerns you are dealing with. Personal strength and control will make a big difference in how team members continue to deal with the difficulties throughout the change process.

Don't forget to listen! Listening sets the stage for success and it acknowledges people and their ideas.

Focus and Visibility

Being able to focus and helping to focus others are great tools for helping facilitate a smooth and effective transition process.

Another great tool is being there, being visible, throughout the change process.

Live the Change

Always keep in mind:

> What you pay attention to happens.
>
> People notice what you spend time on.
>
> People notice what you care about.

Be a Mentor

Helping others with their concerns is what a great leader does. It goes beyond visibility to showing that you care.

Questions and Ideas for Contemplation

If you are currently dealing with a major change at work or are planning a restructuring of your group, spend some time considering how you are going to keep everyone on track throughout the change process, i.e. what do you need to do on a **daily** basis that will show them what is most important.

Also, consider what it will take, both time and effort-wise, to stay on top of how people are feeling, what they are doing, how they are accepting the transition, and whether they are moving ahead. See if you can plan these very important foci into your management schedule.

Other things to consider in maintaining the momentum throughout the change process:

> Your personal integrity, openness, and honesty demonstrate your commitment to your team and to what you believe in

> Your willingness to openly communicate and keep everyone up to snuff with both the good and bad news helps everyone get through difficulties that arise

> Support, encouragement, acknowledgment, etc., really make a difference. (see Chapter 22, "Taking Care of Your People").

> Keep the higher ups apprised, too. Communications work every-which-way.

> Be responsible – do what you say you are going to do, or make sure everyone understands why you couldn't do it. If screw-ups happen, get in there and make a difference and don't pass the buck.

Chapter 8

Losses and Gains

Change Creates Loss

Even positive changes in life, like promotions, create losses. From a leadership perspective you have two primary concerns: what losses you personally must deal with and what losses your team members are dealing with.

In the case of restructuring, adding or losing personnel, etc. the losses may seem minimal on the surface but can have a marked impact emotionally.

Every change has the potential to affect our self-worth, and if we are really truthful, it almost always does.

Self-worth versus Ego

Self-worth means we are comfortable with who we are and are capable of accepting everything that impacts us with self-confidence and self-control. Our egos are at play when we are negatively impacted by what happens to us: defensiveness, complaining, worry, blame, fear, feelings of not being good enough or inadequacy, etc.

Most of us are hit negatively by change. Major change can really hit our self-worth and our egos rise to the occasion to replace our positive self-value.

> If I am in a company that is taken over by another company and my job is eliminated, my self-worth takes a hit. If I think about it logically, there is nothing about this that says anything specific about who I am, how good I am, or what I have done or not done. It is all coming from outside of me. It still will most likely affect how I feel about myself.
>
> My reactions may include shock, disbelief, denial, and

many other emotions. I may also feel, even if for a very brief time, shame, guilt, being vulnerable and/or victimized, etc., all things that show that my self-worth has taken a hit.

We Deal with It

Generally speaking we find ways to work with these emotions and reactions and we quickly reestablish our personal equilibrium and begin to deal with the practical concerns associated with the dramatic change that has blind-sided us. As a manager we also will likely step into our leadership shoes and start making decisions that will help others on our team.

Leadership IS helping others

We and our team members may lose a great deal because of a significant change – like a takeover and/or loss of job. Potentially we will lose not only the work we have done for 'x' number of years, we will also likely lose the familiarity of that work and those surroundings, our friends and coworkers and the relationships we have developed, our home and community relationships if we have to move for a new job, and many other things. The hardest thing to face however is the impact on our self-worth.

This may be the single most important consideration to keep in mind when helping others through the process of change. It takes time, support, encouragement, and caring to help people get back their sense of self-worth, self-confidence, and self-control.

It is also important to remember that self-worth tends to be a personal roller-coaster for everyone during times of significant change and throughout the process of change.

A single change in personnel on a team can impact some of your team members' self-worth a great deal. Make sure you stay on top of how people are feeling, interacting, and adjusting. Provide support and encouragement as it is needed. It is also very useful to let other managers and team members know how much our emotions play a role in being successful throughout the transition process. It will help everyone stay alert to helping everyone else.

Get them to talk about it

Sometimes encouraging people to chat about what they are going through is the best approach for helping them deal with losses and concerns. Informal one-on-ones or small group get-togethers to discuss issues, frustrations, and feelings can ease a good bit of angst. Be willing to follow-up with this on a daily basis when your people are hurting.

Assess what you and they may be losing

Taking a mental (or written) assessment of what we are feeling, thinking and specifically what we are losing because of a significant change in our lives can help us deal with the transition process better. If the change is traumatic, it is especially useful to write down in detail the things we feel we are going to be giving up. This may even be an excellent exercise to have our team members do. When people know what they have to face, it gives them a more solid foundation upon which to make changes and build strategies for working through their losses.

Assess the gains, too

Though it may not seem like it at the time, when we are hard hit by traumatic change, there are always gains, too:

> We learn from what is happening.

> We eventually replace things we lose.

> We may, and often do, find positive outcomes from losses we initially face. Attitude can make a huge difference.

> We create new bonds with new people and may find old bonds are strengthened by what we go through together.

> We ultimately, as we work through the changes successfully, gain self-value, self-confidence, self-control, and patience.

> We gain a greater appreciation for our abilities, particularly to withstand whatever comes at us. We also learn from our weaknesses, if we pay attention.

> We gain more respect for the people we work with and for the people who support and encourage us (especially those at home).

Leading and helping team members to assess their own personal losses and gains and the losses, and gains the team faces, can help everyone face what is happening with greater understanding and self-control throughout the transition process. It can be an eye opening process because our tendency is to only deal with the concerns and problems we personally face.

Questions and Ideas for Contemplation

Make the effort to personally delineate in writing the losses and gains you may likely experience as the result of a major change you are facing. This exercise is very valuable to getting a handle on things and to being able to respond to all the stresses and concerns that arise during the change process. There will be fewer surprises and you will probably handle everything with more control and aplomb.

Make sure you consider having your team members go through the same process. It opens many doors and can empower them to take on much more than they would be able to otherwise in helping the change be successful.

Chapter 9

Grieving Losses

There has been a great deal written about grief and loss. Perhaps the most quoted source is Dr. Kubler-Ross's "Five Stages of Loss/Grief."

Stage 1: Denial

Stage 2: Anger or Resentment

Stage 3: Bargaining

Stage 4: Depression

Stage 5: Acceptance

Paralleling these are Bob Deits' "Steps to Recovery" found in his book *Life After Loss*:

1) Shock and Numbness

2) Denial and Withdrawal

3) Acknowledgment and Pain

4) Adapting and Renewal

As I state in *Difficult Situations: Dealing with Change* I prefer thinking of loss and grief in terms of symptoms. For example:

Anger is a reaction to change; and a 'symptom' that a person is having difficulty at this stage of the process in dealing with the change.

Our initial reaction to change may be shock and numbness. This also can be construed as a symptom of how a person is handling the stress of change.

Work related Loss and Grief

Grief is not Predictable or Controllable

When we lose someone dear to us we know we are going to grieve. When we lose a great deal through change at work, we still need to grieve, but it seems very different because it doesn't equate in any way to losing a loved one. However, our reactions, or the symptoms of loss that we experience, can be similar regardless of the specific type of loss we are experiencing, i.e. we may need to grieve the things we lose (relationships, office space, seniority, etc.) if we are caught in a downsizing.

Certainly the type and intensity of those reactions may be different depending on the type of change/loss we are dealing with. As human beings we need to process the feelings, thoughts, and reactions we have to loss. This is what is meant by grieving, 'the stages of grief,' or the grieving process.

As a leader we expect ourselves, and others expect us, to show courage and fortitude – to be a pillar of strength in times of difficulty. And we need to be. We need to acknowledge our own losses and deal with the emotions, thoughts, and reactions engendered by those losses. We also need to acknowledge that our friends, coworkers, employees, and family, i.e. anyone we interact with, will also be affected by this process. Some may be deeply affected.

We cannot predict how we or anyone else will react to a significant change in our/their work life and the resultant losses we/they will have to face. Some people may be in shock for long periods, others may withdraw and become depressed, or a close colleague may become angry, resentful and act out. We all respond to loss differently. As a leader we hold the huge responsibility for understanding and working with our own responses to loss, as well as the responsibility for helping with the reactions and concerns of our team members.

Pay Attention

Pay attention to how you feel, what you think, and how you are reacting.

Pay attention to the people you are responsible for, too.

Grief symptoms related to loss should be acknowledged and worked through. While we and others may make a credible effort at ignoring or stuffing feelings and reactions, the truth is they will come back to 'bite us,' if we don't face them at some point.

Be open to and willing to admit what you are feeling

Observe yourself: how you feel, what you are thinking, how you react to others and circumstances, particularly stressful times, throughout your daily life

Talk

Talking about loss and the hurt we feel is the best way to face up to what is happening and get through it. It is not going to happen over night or in one sitting. As a leader open your door (and in a sense your arms) and give people a chance to unload. [Don't forget to 'unload' yourself – to people you trust and who are supportive.] Some businesses wisely provide counseling and support services for the staffs when a major change is expected or hits. Find out what is available and encourage your team members to take advantage of all these available services. But don't just leave it in the hands of the professionals – your sense of ownership and caring will make the most difference because you are one of them and involved yourself.

Your willingness as a leader to talk with others about your own feelings and concerns will also help provide a type of support and will be a form of encouragement for others to face up to and work on their reactions as well.

Always keep in mind that the change process, and hence the loss and grieving process, takes time. Some team members may still be dealing with strong feelings and reactions months or a year or more after the change first impacts your group. Part of moving through the change process, often a big part, is acknowledging that our feelings and reactions continue to affect us for some time and that we need to continue to offer support and encouragement to each other throughout if we are to be successful in 'coming out the other side' with a happy, productive team.

Be willing to feel; Encourage others to feel

Sometimes you have to 'be with' your emotions. This is not only okay it is good and necessary to process through them. If you are angry – be angry safely, and acknowledge that you probably have a good reason to feel resentment at what has happened. If you are sad, allow yourself to be sad. If you get depressed, remind yourself that you have suffered losses and are working through the feelings associated with those losses.

Give your people the same support and 'it is okay to feel and work through things' attitude. Sometimes the best thing you can do is commiserate:

> "Bob, I can see you are upset. Let's take a minute to talk about this. I'm upset, too and I think it will do me some good to talk it out with you."

> "Alice you look like you could use a day off. That is just how I felt this morning. Want to take a short break and walk in the atrium to talk about it?"

There are a myriad of ways that you can help others by 'giving them permission' to feel and react. It takes understanding and a willingness to understand. It takes empathy and compassion, with a good bit of kindness thrown in.

Regaining Balance and Control

It seems like we should be able to control what has happened, our reactions and feelings to it, and what is currently happening in our work life. The truth, in times of significant change, is that we really can't. During the change process we are in a sense in an ongoing battle to regain our footing so we can 'get back to normal.' As a leader we do provide some stability for our team members through change. We can also provide understanding and some comfort by helping them understand that these feelings of imbalance and loss of control and resultant reactions are normal and need to be processed throughout the transition. Encourage them to work with their own feelings and thoughts and to share with others what they are processing.

Working equals progress

Working with our grief and losses means we are getting on with our work and lives. The more actively we and our team members are involved in getting through the feelings and concerns that arise, the better the transition process.

The tendency is to pay attention to these concerns for the first few weeks after the initial impact of the change and then we slowly let things slide. The process of change, all aspects of that process, takes a considerable length of time to get through. Your people will be feeling and reacting to the stresses of the change process for a long time. So will you.

Pay attention!

How do we know we have arrived?

Jumping ahead quite a few Chapters, this question is often on our minds when we are working through change, grief, and loss. Unfortunately there is no real finish line. The goal is to reach a point where we, our team members, and all the people we interact with have reestablished our sense of ownership, effectiveness, productivity, and balance within the organization and with what we do.

Is that possible? Yes, if you are willing, as a leader and as an employee to realize that change is really a constant part of our lives and the flexibility and creativity we need to deal with ongoing change is part of what we learn when we deal with major changes in our work life.

Questions and Ideas for Contemplation

Consider a recent (or current) change you have dealt with.

What emotions, thoughts, reactions did you have?

How did you feel about the things you lost as a result?

How did you deal with them?

Did you grieve your losses in the broadest meaning of grief and the 'stages' or 'symptoms' of grief?

Can you remember the reactions of some of your employees and colleagues?

Can you think of ways in which you could have helped others with their feelings and concerns?

Chapter 10

Obstacles During the Change Process

There are two primary obstacles you face during the change process: bureaucracy and resistance.

Bureaucracy

In Chapter Six, we discussed dealing with bureaucracy at some length. Here are a few other key points:

> Bureaucracy is something we have to deal with throughout the change process. It is amazing how many obstacles can be placed in our way, even by the higher ups who created, instigated, and/or encouraged changes in the first place.

> Always have a clear, cogent, well-thought out plan. Be ready and willing to answer questions, do more background work if needed, revise, and compromise if it is acceptable within the scope of what you want to accomplish.

> Be positive, even if you are frustrated. It sometimes takes a good bit of cajoling to bring people around. Remember: "Negativity Never Helps" (*A Perfect Day*, Koob)

> Be patient and keep at it. It is easy to lose momentum and to get frustrated. Always go back to what you strongly believe in. If the changes you want to make have to do with the ultimate quality and effectiveness of your team, then keep those values and goals at the forefront of your efforts. AND make sure that whoever is heading the roadblock to what you want to accomplish understands that quality and effectiveness ARE the purposes behind the changes you want to make.

> Be creative: in your ideas and in how you present them. Sometimes the easiest way around an obstacle is to tackle

the idea from a different perspective or to couch it in different terms.

Help your boss (or other obstacle creator) to own part of the solution (and part of the problem). In the final analysis it really doesn't matter who gets the credit, as long as you get to where you want to be. 'Being right' will not make you happy – being good (quality and effectiveness) may.

When you need to push, be willing to make hard decisions. Weigh options against your goals and the potential risks.

> Sitting around becoming increasingly frustrated is no fun at all.

Resistance

Resistance comes from people and it is a natural reaction to change, especially to change that comes at us from without. Interestingly, we also often resist change that we instigate ourselves. There is just something about 'how things are' that is more comfortable than 'how things are going to be, if...'

Much of the typical bureaucracy we run into is the result of stubborn people adhering rigidly to rules, policies, procedures, and the way they like things to be. The key ideas below can go a long way to helping overcome roadblocks being clung to by other people in the system.

Dealing with Resistance: Key Ideas

Understand

When we make an effort to understand the resistance and what is driving it, we stand a much better chance of working through it successfully with that person. **Attention** and **understanding** go a long way toward getting others to work with you on getting past concerns.

Identifying what the resistance is and delineating it as clearly as possible helps in two ways:

> The resistor understands what they are doing much more clearly, and it is not unusual for them to discover the fact

that they were unknowingly causing part of the concern. (Hint: they are much more likely to blame you up to that point.)

You have a much better handle on how to deal with the concern.

By understanding specifically what you are up against, you can change the dynamics of the resistance and your interactions. With that knowledge you can more easily create venues for getting past these concerns.

Paying attention to another person and acknowledging their importance also changes the dynamics of resistance in most cases. As a result:

They feel more a part of the whole team effort

They feel that they are important to the change process.

They will notice that you notice, i.e., every time you have the opportunity to reinforce your interest in them is time well spent.

You will learn more readily where they are coming from and what they want.

Ask

Understanding is possible only if you are willing to ask and listen to another person's ideas, thoughts, and feelings, and when you observe their reactions when they respond. They will tell you their concerns if you pay attention, are patient, and are genuinely interested.

Be Patient

Some people, especially passive and passive-aggressive types, require a great deal of patience. Even if you have made the effort to understand their concerns, they may still resist. Let them. Your patience and understanding will pay off in the long run. Don't expect all your personnel to jump on board just because you have great ideas. Some people will make up their own minds over time. Your key is to show them, throughout the change process, that your goals are valid and critical to who you are and what you want the team to be. Be persistent, patiently persistent, with what you want to accomplish with these types.

Help them get vested in the problem;

help them get vested in the solution.

(See Chapter 4)

The more a person understands why, how, when, where, how much, etc. the more likely they will start to become part of the solution and lose their resistance to change. You might be able to show them that they don't have any choice and that whatever they want and are concerned about doesn't matter, because based on the agenda you have received from above in the chain, things ARE going to change. You still want to work with them to get them involved in the whys and wherefores.

What they understand, what they have input into, what they have the opportunity to strive for because it is for the common and their own good in the long run, will help them get involved and on board.

Communicate

Communicate your values, the qualities you are striving for, and your goals in every way possible. You create the aura of **what can be** through your communications and your actions. (See also Chapters 3 and 4) People will change because they want to change. When they have a clear picture of who you are and what is important to you, they will get on your 'A train' much sooner. Most people respond positively to a strong, positive, value-centered leader. Some will take longer than others, but positive, open communications will help them change too.

Communicate wisely

How you talk with people is just as important as what you are talking about. Positive, open communications set the stage for how the members of your team will interact with each other, with you, and with all those other people from across the matrixes that affect your team.

Have problems, concerns?

Get them out in the open and get people discussing them.

Some managers wonder why they have such a hard time getting information from their team members. Typically it takes a hard look at how we are communicating ourselves before we can realize where that resistance is coming from. The laws haven't changed much since we were children – we do what we see, i.e. what is reinforced on a regular basis.

> Do you want to have more open and honest communications in your group?

Then take a look at your style and change what you need to change. And don't forget, you have to get out there amongst the troops to make a difference.

Negativity

'There is one in every bunch,' is not too far from the truth. Leaders need to be concerned with how people feel and what they are spreading throughout the team and the organization by their communications with others. Negativity can quickly undermine efforts to make significant positive changes within a group.

Two key ideas relative to negativity in personnel:

> Everyone will have negative feelings, worries, stresses, thoughts, and reactions during major disruptions. Expect it. Expect to work with people on these concerns.

> Some people, there IS at least one in every bunch, will become the catalyst for ongoing negativity. It is important to deal with 'doom and gloomers' quickly and effectively.

Dealing with negativity will be the focus of the next Chapter.

Positivity

Your positivity and your recognition and reward of positivity in others can add immeasurably to the ability of your team to get through obstacles that threaten to block your forward momentum through the change process.

Praise what is right with your team. Recognize the contributions people are making and the momentum they have created. Others will want to come on board as a result.

Questions and Ideas for Contemplation

Most resistance can be reduced or eliminated through positive communications and by the passage of time. The thoughts in this Chapter can facilitate and expedite getting past obstacles and resistances. Always keep in mind that **what you do**, **what you say**, and **what you believe in** are the most important tools you have in working with others and in dealing with change.

Do you have a specific issue or concern you would like to address? We are here and we listen. You can always contact us at www.difficultpeople.org with your ideas, questions, scenarios, and comments. Select the response link and send us an e-mail. You should hear from us within 48 hours depending on the volume of requests.

Chapter 11

Dealing with Negativity

Change does tend to create negative emotions and reactions. People feel bad. They want to blame someone for their problems and for what is happening. Things can look pretty dismal if the change is affecting jobs, families, work relationships, etc. Leadership means working with and through the good AND the bad.

Most negative reactions and concerns are short-lived and come and go throughout the change process. We all are impacted in different ways. I may be down one day, and vibrant and forward-looking the next. I may be worried sick, resentful, upset, and/or sad about what has happened or I may weather things effectively one day and not the next.

Some reactions to major disruptions can affect people for long(er) periods of time. Length of time has to do with the significance of the change to the individual, their psychological make-up and resilience at the time, and whether the person/persons are making the effort to work through their emotions and reactions with support and encouragement.

The good news is that generally over time most of us get through these negative feelings and begin to regain our composure and balance, especially if we are willing to work at it. We set our teeth and dig in to finding solutions for ourselves. We also make an effort to get our minds back to our work and we start working through things with our teammates.

We make do; and eventually things get better.

Dealing with Negative Reactions

Leaders need to stay on top of how their people are feeling and they need to understand that people will be dealing with negative emotions and reactions for some time. Support, encouragement, and the ability to listen compassionately play a very important role in helping team members through difficult change and the emotions and reactions engendered by change and loss.

Shock, Panic, Fear

Initially it is very common for most people to experience confusion, shock, and numbness when a major change suddenly hits home. These reactions can be followed by feelings of panic and ongoing underlying fear about the future. These are normal reactions that usually give way fairly quickly in most people to determination and action.

Leaders can help their team members the most through these early reactions by being available, acting professionally and with integrity in all their interactions with them, and by showing compassion and concern. When we share a bit of ourselves, we empower others to share and we show them that they aren't alone.

> "I really understand what you are going through, Steve. I feel like I've been hit by a sledgehammer myself. I guess we are all wondering what will happen next."

> "You aren't alone in this, Jean. I know I am feeling pretty tense these days myself waiting for the next bomb to drop."

There is certainly cause for concern if these reactions/symptoms persist. Professional help may be warranted, see below.

Anger, Upset, Irritability

Difficult change causes upset. Worry, anxiety, and stress can lead to angry outbursts, irritability, and even aggressive behavior. Leaders can make a difference by paying attention and stepping in when needed.

Sometimes the simplest approach is the best:

> "Alice, you seem angry about something. Do you want to talk?"

> "Bob, several people have made comments about your seeming a bit more uptight than normal. Can I help?"

These simple statements acknowledge the other person, let them know that you and others have noticed how they feel, show concern, and open the door to communications. They can go a long way to alleviating problems that can become much more serious over time. When we broach these types of issues in a kind and forthright manner, we make a difference.

Complaining sessions can also be useful if the mood is proactive. Let everyone have their say about how they feel. Let them get things out into the open. Encourage them to avoid blame and judgments, take responsibility for themselves and their own feelings, and to discuss solutions. When people know how their colleagues are feeling it often helps to temper their own reactions and lets them know that they aren't alone. It also gives them the opportunity to identify people they may want to share their thoughts and feelings with a bit further. Note: People will gripe anyway – making it an 'event' helps get it all out in the open.

Disillusioned, Sad, Depressed/Lowered Affect

Many of the ideas above are relevant to people who are feeling down. The most important tool is to get people talking about how they feel. Being isolated and feeling unsupported increases the likelihood that people will fall into bouts of low self-esteem and poor motivation.

Take opportunities, especially if you can do so intermittently and spontaneously, to acknowledge people for their contributions, to recognize and celebrate accomplishments, and to otherwise give them the chance to let their 'hair down.' A bit of fun and celebration can go a long way toward alleviating the doldrums through the long transition process.

Worry, Feeling Vulnerable

Feeling worried is one of the most common reactions to change and the stressful situations engendered by change. It is normal, and can even be healthy, as it helps us pay attention to things that need to be thought-out. Worry becomes a problem when people perseverate about negative thoughts to the extent that they begin a downward spiral of going over the same negative feelings over and over with no resolution.

Talking it out with another person can help, but the best technique may be writing feelings and thoughts down. When we put things into some concrete form, they seem to become more real, less uncontrollable, and we can then work toward brainstorming solutions (also useful to do in writing).

Vulnerability is a common initial reaction and a feeling that tends to be fairly omnipresent throughout the change process until people start to feel they are mostly back on their feet. It can be exacerbated by leaders who fail to share information regarding the change process in a timely manner, who try to hide bad news from their team members, or who pass the buck when it comes to delivering bad news. The responsible leader can have a huge impact on how employees feel about themselves. While you may not be able to change bad news or avoid some of the problems that occur because of change, you can keep people informed and make sure you let them know that you are out there going to bat for them at every turn.

Resentment, Betrayal, Feeling Victimized

Stuff happens. Bad stuff happens to good people. We don't have to look too far to see the results of poor and dishonest management (recent corporate debacles come to mind). It is certainly possible that a change that is impacting you and your people is not fair and could have been handled better. You and they, however, still have to deal with what is.

Resentment, especially, can cause long term resistance and problems in working through change. Getting it out in the open and helping people talk about how they feel is the best technique for dealing with these often 'underground' and closely guarded feelings. The more open your leadership style, the more you get around and talk with people, the more likely you will be able to get a handle on these types of feelings before they can create major concerns.

Overwhelmed, Frustrated

Change can hit hard and it can hit fast. Once it hits, it can go railroading onward without any consideration for what we can handle, what we are supposed to be accomplishing, and how we are supposed to deal with all these new concerns and problems.

Break things into small pieces: the more manageable the tasks set before you and your team throughout the change process the more success you will all have and the better people will feel. Sometimes things do have to be put on the back burner. Make sure everyone understands the priorities – they should rest in your values, the qualities you aspire for as individuals and as a team, and in your primary vision and commitment; they should rest first and foremost with your people. Anything else may have to be dealt with as time allows.

Other emotions and reactions

There are many types of feelings and reactions that we could discuss in this section. The best ideas and tools for helping team members (and yourself) work through them are above. Always try to keep in mind the following:

> You are dealing with people: their feelings and thoughts. Treat them as you feel you should be treated.

> Open communications are the fundamental key to success.

> Caring, concern, and kindness go a long way.

> How you present yourself as a leader throughout the change process can make all the difference. Get back to basics; get back to integrity, honesty, ownership, and responsibility.

> Did I mention you should care?

Really negative people

Unfortunately the old adage is usually true: there is one in every bunch and one can become two, four, five, etc., if these concerns are not dealt with quickly. If you are new to a team as the result of the change process and haven't built a rapport with them, this may be even more of a challenge.

Negativity can permeate a group very quickly, especially when times are tough. Change is one of those ideal breeding grounds for the doomsayers, blamers, and complainers.

Important: There are many sections throughout the difficultpeople.org literature that talk about working with negativity/negative people. See specifically our signature books, *Understanding and Working with Difficult People*, and *Me! A Difficult Person?*

Nip it in the bud.

The best tactic for ongoing and rooted negativity is to bring it out into the open.

> "Mark, I have heard a fair number of negative comments from you in meetings and in passing. I've also received some complaints from others. Let's sit down and talk about this because I am very concerned about how you are doing personally and the impact you are having on others."

Be straightforward, listen to everything they have to say, including their denials (very likely), with an open, receptive demeanor. The key is that they know you are aware. That basic knowledge changes the whole dynamics of the situation for them and for you.

Stay positive and offer them positive alternatives and choices. Get them onboard an activity in which they can shine. Pay attention to them, not so much to keep track of what they are doing, but to offer support, encouragement, and positive feedback for accomplishments. Negative behavior is rooted in negative self-worth. You can't change that overnight, but you can make a difference. The key is to stay on top of this. Any slippage on your part can leave the door open for them to revert back to old habits. It does take some time investment, but the payoffs can be huge. You may, over the long haul, gain a valuable, dedicated employee, and you will save yourself and your team members many headaches.

Professional Help

Problems and concerns arise with personnel that you are not equipped to handle. A consistently troublesome employee might benefit a great deal from professional coaching. A severely depressed team member could probably use medical evaluation and counseling.

Get help for your personnel when it is warranted. Be sure you remain aware of their involvement in your unit and how they are doing, because that will make a big difference over the long haul.

Leadership often comes down to making choices. Weigh the possibilities and make the best possible choices for your team members, for your team, and for yourself.

Questions and Ideas for Contemplation

Your team members will experience many emotions throughout the <u>whole</u> change process. Negative affect comes from our loss of self-worth and self-confidence, our sense of being out of control, and the imbalance we feel in our work and life. One of the most important things you can do for your team members is to acknowledge these concerns. Let them know you understand and are there to help.

Avoiding judgment and blame are difficult to manage in the face of ongoing negativity. Consider ways in which you can deal with negative affect and still maintain a positive, proactive approach. Your impact will be much more effective.

Chapter 12

Failing Up

"Failing up" is all attitude. It is making sure everyone knows and buys into the following:

It is okay to make mistakes or fail at a task or goal...

if...

You and the team learn and gain from it.

It is not about purposefully failing at something, though there are instances where a bit of purposeful mistake making will eliminate possibilities and narrow the field toward eventual success. It is also not about being slack on quality and effort. If anything, it encourages high quality and extraordinary effort. It is about taking well-thought out risks and chances (see Sections 73 through 79 in *Honoring Work and Life*: Creativity; Innovation; Flexibility; Experiment; Risk-Taking; Fluidity; and Chances.]

This idea comes from a interpretation of ideas I read in Tom Peters' books, most notably *Re-imagine: Business Excellence in A Disruptive Age* and a little gem of a book he recommended, *Whoever Makes the Most Mistakes Wins,* by Richard Farson and Ralph Keyes.

Non-stop Change

This idea is particularly useful in today's business climate where change in some form or another is always impacting our teams and organizations. When leaders create a work environment that encourages a certain amount of risk-taking with the motivational and intellectual caveat that there is much to be gained from failure, a team is empowered to try new ideas, remain flexible in dealing with the impact of changes that hit the group, and find ways to make the most of the efforts that don't work.

Fluidity is a good descriptive term for this type of operation. People know they have a certain amount of freedom and the responsibility that goes with that freedom and they take it and run with it. It creates an openness to new ideas. It gets people sharing and talking up what they are doing and the potential of the ideas they are trying. It creates a flow of information that otherwise might be stifled because "We are not allowed to fail," or we are "Afraid to fail because it will affect our evaluation process."

Eliminate the judgments

It is so easy to judge others. If we actually take the time to pay attention to our thought patterns, it is easy to see how many hundreds of judgments we make every day.

> "She's wearing brown shoes with that green dress. Yuck.."

> "Why doesn't he do something about that mess of a workstation?"

> "He sure goes through a lot of paper every week." And so on.

When we make these judgments in regards to someone's work, and we do make them frequently, how does it affect our perspective of someone? How does this affect our attitude about what they do and how they do it? When we verbalize judgments, what messages are we sending?

If our attitude is anything less than,

> "Good try, Bob. Your experiment told us a lot about that particular technique. Where do you want to take this next," we may be discouraging, demeaning, and otherwise creating a less than open and accepting attitude about taking chances.

Everything we, as leaders, do at work reflects in our group attitude. If we are more open and accepting of risk-taking, if we allow our team players to 'fail up,' most of them will also develop the same positive, 'let's make something out of this opportunity,' attitude.

Eliminate the blame

> "It is Bob's fault the project isn't done yet. He's been tinkering with that new gizmo idea for months."

Whoever said this may be right; but being right and pointing fingers doesn't solve problems or concerns. If Bob is onto something and really feels that he is close to a breakthrough in working with a new product, his experimentation and the resultant slow-down may be the catalyst for the next blockbuster idea.

If he's just dawdling along and not accomplishing anything worthwhile, but following nebulous whims, then this is a personnel problem that needs to be addressed. However, even in such a case, pointing fingers and assigning blame doesn't accomplish anything. Making some changes to facilitate the ongoing project development might be in order and so will helping Bob get motivated onto a worthwhile project that helps the team goals (into the right seat on the bus).

Blame permeates teams/people that have little flexibility, are only success oriented, have little self-worth, and are afraid to make mistakes. It is also frequently manifested on teams where the leader is always assigning blame and rarely taking responsibility or ownership.

Leaders often have to balance creativity and productivity. Keeping open to new ideas and informed at every level are ways we can make wise decisions. There are almost always positive, non-judgmental ways we help people stay on track in an open-spirited environment.

Fail Up because...

It helps create and keep momentum going through the change process and it gives a team the flexibility to deal with constant changes that impact the group.

It helps create a much more positive and accepting attitude throughout the group.

It encourages new ideas and the sharing of ideas.

People have more fun.

People find more ways to succeed because they are taking intelligent risks and are willing to take chances.

It helps create positive self-worth, self-confidence, and self-control and ownership (acceptance of responsibility for one's actions).

It helps people develop more open and fluid working relationships, where they are empowered to help each other make a difference.

It empowers people to take a proactive role in dealing with non-stop change.

Treat everyone as if They are on the "A" Team

Motivation has a great deal to do with how people feel about themselves. When we give everyone the chance to prove themselves, almost all of them will. Treat them as stars and they will make every effort to be a star. And always empower them to 'Fail Up,' when they are working hard.

It IS all about YOUR attitude

Your leadership sets the stage. If you aren't used to giving leeway to others, allowing players more responsibility, creating a more accepting attitude with far less judgment and blame, then you have some work to do.

> It takes paying attention to how you interact with team members.

> It takes being aware of what you say and do that can be construed as limiting, judgmental, or blaming.

> It takes making an effort to present your thoughts and ideas in as positive a way as possible.

> It takes talking (and living what you talk) – as often as possible about what 'Failing Up' means to your group – that making gains from mistakes and failures is a good way to look at our work.

Questions and Ideas for Contemplation

I preach creativity, flexibility, curiosity in everything I do educationally, but I am also very big on quality. The two are not mutually exclusive. It is well worth spending some time on two endeavors related to this concept:

Think about where you stand with regard to being able to give your team players more responsibility and flexibility. What would it take for you to relax your current attitude?

Spend a committed week paying attention to how your attitude, thoughts, actions, and communications limit your group's attitude, openness, and energy. [Hint: By far, a huge majority of us do this, though we are rarely aware of it unless we make this effort.]

Then make the effort to stay on top of how your attitude and actions as a leader affect your team players and the overall tenor of your group. This does take a concerted effort, but the rewards over the long haul in your learning about yourself and how you impact others, and how they respond to you, are tremendous.

Chapter 13

Creating Possibilities

We often look at major changes in work and in life as difficulties we have to face and get through. This can be particularly true if the change we are facing creates considerable angst and turmoil and if it results in people having to make difficult adjustments because they have lost a job, changed positions, are facing a takeover and a move, etc.

Change also creates possibilities. Sometimes it creates golden opportunities. A lot has to do with how we face change, our attitude.

Approaching Change and the Change Process

When the first of the dust settles and we gain at least a bit of a perspective on what has happened, is happening, and what the future may portend, most people begin to adjust. We also begin to accept changes that need to be made and make an effort to deal with the stress and concerns that we are facing.

Sometimes our attitude is:

"How much more can the world pile on my shoulders?"

Sometimes it is,

"I guess I'll just have to make the most of this, like everything else."

Or perhaps it could be,

"I can handle this, and I'm going to come out of this okay."

If we are really extraordinary, we might think,

"Wow, I really needed this kick in the butt to wake me up. I'm going to take this opportunity and run with it."

That last one sounds nice doesn't it? Also, probably a bit 'pie-in-the-sky,' because most of us are still dealing with our emotions and our reactions to what has happened and is happening.

Whatever your beliefs are, there is something great about approaching life with an attitude of positivity. Whether you believe that providence affects your life and sets tasks for you so that you are learning and growing from the difficulties you face, or whether you just view life as 'the luck of the draw,' you still have the opportunity to choose a negative, 'woe is me' attitude OR a 'I'm going to make the most of this and kick some butt,' approach.

> I spent too many years of my life reacting and fighting things that came at me. I have had a whole lot more fun and been much more proactive about my own life since I made the choice to own who I was and what I was doing, becoming. It was all about what I was telling myself and what I was believing about circumstances.

Choose wisely. As a leader it affects your whole group and all the people you interact with at work.

Creating possibilities from change

Once we have accepted the challenges of the change(s) we are facing, we can take the whole change process a step further and create a whole new work life from the ashes of the old. This can be, if we choose to make it that way, exciting, enervating, challenging, and motivating for us and for our team members.

Besides attitude adjustment it takes curiosity, willingness to innovate, supporting creativity and experimentation, and an openness to taking some chances. These are all concepts that a leader can help foster in his/her team.

Reward creativity and creative thinking

People buy into what you pay attention to and what you talk about. People do what they get rewarded to do. As a leader, nurture creativity and innovation by rewarding the process as much as, or more than, the outcomes.

> "Yes, John, that is the kind of thinking I want to see around here."

"Great start, Elise. Go ahead and follow up on this and see where it leads."

Creative leaders learn to recognize and reward even crazy ideas. Non-judgmental brainstorming sessions can be fun and give everyone the opportunity to add ideas to the mix. Some of the wildest ideas in business history have become huge successes. They don't even have to make any sense. Who would have thought thousands and thousands of 'Pet Rocks' would have been sold. [Ever wonder what became of all those old pets?] Even if you don't manage to come up with the next blockbuster for your team/company, everyone will have more fun, ideas will generate more ideas, and a more open, creative attitude will permeate your group.

Keep in mind that often the best rewards are verbal thanks or praise, and the simple things we do for others – like a pat-on-the-back e-mail or a kind word.

Got a problem?

Most of the time, the solutions to problems that arise are not very far away in the ideas of people on your team. Give them the opportunity and motivation to kick things around and be willing to pay close attention to what transpires. A good many trials and tribulations will get solved much more easily than by you or your crack committee spending hours worrying or stewing over them.

Don't just sell the problem and the solution, be willing to give them the challenge of thinking about and dealing with the problem. Too often leaders shoulder many things that others may have the inclination, the insight, and the energy to tackle. [Hint: This is one of the reasons managers have time management concerns. See Chapter 19]

Great leaders give team members the opportunity and responsibility to try.

Get creative with creativity

We are all capable of thinking up creative ways to get team members involved and to get them creatively working on problems and concerns. Create your own venues for developing ideas, accepting and working on challenges, and for facilitating experimentation of ideas.

Listen

Open up to the possibilities. I wonder how many potentially great ideas have gone by the wayside because a manager just brushed them off without really making the effort to understand what was being proposed. We all have our prejudices and biases. Don't let them get in the way of listening to what a fellow employee has to offer. Only when you have given them this courtesy, will you be able to say, "I don't think so," kindly, without doing major damage to their personal creative energy and willingness to explore new ideas.

Since I decided life wasn't so much a battle against the forces that be and more of a series of challenges for me to make the most of, I have had many serendipitous events and things fall into my lap. Or was it that I just had my eyes and ears open and was able to take advantage of random occurrences? It doesn't really matter. I am having a whole lot more fun now.

Questions and Ideas for Contemplation

Creativity is humanity's gift to themselves and the world. We are all capable of being creative, it just takes thinking beyond what is. We can all do that. If you think you are not very creative, then spend some time thinking creatively. You will likely be very surprised at yourself!

Creativity is one of the best tools you have, and your team members have, to successfully navigate the many difficulties encountered in the change process. Creativity fosters motivation, energy, and fun. What is not to like?

Encourage brainstorming sessions. Write random ideas from everyone on a board or in a notebook for future reference.

Afraid things will get out-of-hand? Even if they do, you are not going anywhere just yet, let them have some fun and then bring the focus back to the vision, plans, strategies, and goals – oh well! We all have to have a little of the mundane in our lives.

Chapter 14

Vision, Plans, Strategies, and Goals

Before we discuss specific types of business-related change, it is important to further delineate the process of change and how to prepare for moving ahead through that long transition. In Chapter 4 we discussed the significance of Vision through change. Immediately below is a reiteration of a key idea from that Chapter.

Keep it Simple!

The more complex your vision of the future

and your strategies to get to that future,

the more difficult will be the change process.

Ideally what you envision should be based on key values: quality, ownership, persistence, etc. Whatever you and they can grab onto as worthwhile goals. Everything else, i.e. specific strategies and goals, are the means to achieving these key ideas/ideals.

Whenever possible break strategies and goals into easily and quickly achievable bites. As emphasized earlier, nothing engenders success and movement like success and movement.

Always come back to the most basic concepts:

> What is my purpose?

> What am I trying to accomplish?

Vision expanded

Initially the most important 'vision' a leader needs to consider in dealing with change is one that gets people on board what needs to happen and what will likely happen.

If the change is instigated by the team leader or by the organization to enhance operations, improve productivity, reduce costs, or otherwise make the group more efficient and effective, then the goal of the vision is to get them to buy into why this is necessary and beneficial in the long run.

If the change results from a merger or acquisition, major downsizing, or other major organizational change, then getting people on board 'the vision,' i.e. the reasons the company was impelled to make these changes, is going to be a tough sell. It is still possible, and something a wise leader will want to address even at the team level. However, keep in mind that people are most concerned with, "What is going to happen to me?" And if that means they are going to lose their jobs, be moved to another state, get 'demoted,' or lose pay and benefits so the company can stay afloat (though the chairman just got a 30 million dollar bonus), then they aren't going to buy into the corporate vision.

The job of the team or group leader then becomes, "How can we all make the best of this situation? How can we do the best for everyone on this team and come out of this with the best possible results?"

This type of vision sets the stage for plans, strategies, and goals.

Plans and Strategies: The Big Picture

It IS important for large organizations to have delineated plans, strategies, and goals when they are going through a major change, i.e. a merger. From the top management teams down through the lines and matrixes including Human Resources departments, legal departments, finance/budget, etc., consideration needs to be given to what is going to happen, how it will be handled, and what needs to happen to facilitate the joining of two disparate organizations. The more that is left to chance, the more concerns and difficulties will arise.

This book is not concerned with detailing the plans and strategies of huge corporations and their top management teams. This book focuses on, at the roots, what your team, line, matrix, 'in-the-trenches' managers, your front-line managers, can do to facilitate change in their groups, i.e. how can they help their people come out of this most successfully.

The Best Possible Outcomes: Selling the Future

In developing a vision of the future, the first consideration should be trying to develop a picture of what **can be**. This may be wishful thinking, because often when we are dealing with major changes in an organization, we don't know right away, or perhaps for some time, what the future may hold. Go ahead and do some wishing.

Remember – getting people moving is critical to being successful through the change process.

How to Sell the Future

If this is an internal restructuring and you hold the keys, let them know what your final desired outcomes are and get them talking about them and how the team can get there.

> Brainstorm possibilities: encourage them to consider both good and bad scenarios and 'what ifs.'

> Talk about it – get it out in the open. People are going to talk anyway, might as well open the doors so that everyone benefits.

> Encourage your people to make preparations for a wide variety of possibilities.

> Think of alternatives and choices they may have for both positive and negative scenarios, i.e. help people get their resumes in order and encourage them to begin to contact recruiters, other companies, etc., This will be appropriate if there is a chance jobs will be eliminated.

> Provide as many resources as possible to facilitate all of the above: books and other reference materials, contacts, coaching if feasible, etc.

Throughout the change process make sure the doors of communication remain open. People will often be able to handle even the most difficult issues of change and loss if they feel they have some means of control and input.

When you do know what the final outcome is going to be, then you can begin to make specific plans, strategies, and set goals for your team.

Plans and Strategies: Moving Through the Change Process

It is very helpful for leaders and their teams to design and delineate plans and strategies for the change process. Once you know what the end result will look like, i.e. the dust has settled and everyone knows how the change will generally impact them, you can get your people involved with this process.

Keep in mind that typically in major organizational change and restructuring that the plans, strategies, and goals handed down from above are often 'way up there' and seem to have little consideration for people as individuals who are trying to deal with serious personal considerations. There may be an effort by senior management and human resources departments to do a great deal and to provide resources that people can access, but it is you, the manager who deals with your people on a daily basis, who has to create the understanding, the sense of caring and ownership, and the vision for moving through change.

Much of the work you do in developing plans and strategies depends on the size of your group. If you are working with a group of twenty or less, you may want to get everyone together to literally 'hash out' many of these issues. If your group is larger, consider a committee to work on ideas, town hall meetings to share concerns, and other venues to gather input. Help your managers understand and get up to speed on the impact change can have on their team members. Make sure they understand the need for personal contact and the communication skills needed to facilitate change.

Also, make sure, whatever size group or level you are dealing with that you are personally involved. Don't just make assignments and let things go as they will. People need support, direction, and encouragement throughout the change process and especially during the early organizational phases.

It Ain't a One Shot Deal

Whatever you and your team members come up with in regards to plans and strategies, remember you are working through a CHANGE process. Things change frequently and adjustments need to be made often. Revisiting and revising plans and strategies, and even adjusting final outcomes, throughout the transition is smart management. It not only makes sure that things stay focused toward the best possible outcomes and means of getting there, it keeps everyone involved in the change process and helps keep the momentum going.

Always bring all of this back to the fundamental truths, values, qualities that you and your team aspire to. Plans, strategies, and goals that don't have these as the foundation are not going to be embraced by your team. Whenever possible keep these in the picture and at the forefront of what is happening and what your people are thinking about. If people are discussing (arguing?) a specific issue related to a planned strategy, you can always ask the question,

> "What is the best possible choice for us to achieve the quality (pick a value) we stand for?"

Goals

Goals are wrapped around plans and strategies, and vice versa. During major disruptions they may initially be 'pie in the sky,' 'this is really what we would like to see happen,' dreams. That is okay. Getting people, who may very well be in shock, confused, and upset focusing in on possibilities, will give them something to think about. It will give them some direction and momentum.

Be practical, too.

Worrying will probably see to the rest. What is important is to bring it all out into the open where people can help each other deal with their stresses and concerns.

When more is known, as the process of change moves ahead, more specific, proactive goals can be envisioned and worked toward.

Short term plans, strategies, and goals

Helping team members and teams be successful throughout the change process is critical because there is nothing like success to get them moving in the right direction. Though you may discuss and work through long-term plans and strategies, helping people reach intermediate goals is also very important. These may be things that you, as a leader, simply recognize because it is needed at the time, or they can be specifically delineated in the planning sessions.

Give everyone the opportunity to feel good about what is happening along the way. It will make a big difference in keeping the momentum going and in keeping people focused 'on the ball.'

K.I.S.

Keep it Simple. If it is, people will be more likely to keep at it and be able to focus on what needs to be done. The more complex, the more likely you will spend a good deal of time and effort keeping things going throughout the transition process.

Finally

It is about making a difference. Ask yourself this question every day:

"What difference do I (we) want to make (today)?"

You might want to ask this of your team members every day, too.

Questions and Ideas for Contemplation

The development of intermediate and short-term goals are important to moving successfully through change.

What types of success could you recognize along the way if one of your final outcomes was to increase the efficiency of your group?

Or to improve communications throughout your line?

These are the types of questions that are valuable to ask and answer. Otherwise 'increasing efficiency' and 'improving communications' are only 'way out there,' or 'Oh, yeah, that is a great idea,' visions and goals.

Try to spend some time thinking about your desired outcomes, your plans and strategies for getting there, and then brainstorm ways to make these meaningful by setting up successes along the way.

Chapter 15

The 'Little' Changes that Matter

You lose a person from your team and must replace them or there is a hiring freeze and you have to 'make do.'

You have two new hires and they need to be assimilated into the team.

You have just taken over a new group because of a promotion.

You have been moved from one division to another and are now heading up a new team.

Your budget has been slashed, but you are expected to 'carry on.'

Your boss has been promoted or leaves for another job and someone else comes in.

You want to change the dynamics and effectiveness of your team and you instigate a team restructuring plan.

All Change Matters; All Change affects People

Each of the 'small' changes above will make a difference to you, your team, and everyone your team impacts. You could probably easily think of a half dozen or more other 'minor' changes you have been through in the past year or two.

> What were your concerns?
>
> What bumps in the road did you encounter?
>
> Do you think you could have been more successful in dealing with these changes if you had tried other techniques or approaches?

This Chapter (this book) is about ideas and tools to help.

Positivity breeds Positivity

And Negativity breeds Negativity.

I start with this, because many managers deal with change, loss, problems, and concerns, 'seriously.' Unfortunately many people, very likely including some or most of your team members, may construe 'serious' with demanding, negative, poor or limited tight-lipped communications, and rigidity.

Some managers are great at pretty much everything except relating at a grass roots level to the concerns of their team members. It doesn't have to be 'touchy-feely;' but it helps immensely if you can start the process of change with an effort to understand how people will be affected, make encouragement and support part of your early and continued agenda, and to have an attitude of positive commitment to working through the change.

Your attitude, whatever it may be, will rub off. What most of us don't realize, MOST OF THE TIME, is how others see us. Be sure to pay attention to yourself and to how you appear to impact your team members, colleagues, and boss AND don't be afraid to ask them.

Know yourself – any negativity you show will impact other members of your team!

We have already said most of this

Many of the ideas already presented in this book are fundamental to being successful with these types of changes. Here are some key ideas revisited (and a few new ones, too) with more emphasis toward team building through change.

Know your people

Whether you are taking over a new group or assimilating new members into your group, getting to know your personnel immediately if not sooner is critical to your success and a successful transition for everyone.

> For example: When I was interviewing for new University administrative positions, before I went for an interview I would get on-line and visit the departmental website and learn everything I could about the personnel in that

department. I would memorize names of faculty and staff, review whatever information was available, and look up research abstracts and publications. People noted and appreciated that effort when I got to the interview.

Communications (see also Chapter 17)

Open up, get information out as soon as possible, and keep people informed at every opportunity. Don't assume that people know, that the grapevine will take care of it, or that the information isn't important to someone. It is much better to let people know what is going on than to let things fester behind the scenes.

Communications are two way. The more opportunities you give your team players to communicate their concerns, ideas, feelings, and reactions (how the change is affecting them), the more you will learn and the better you will able to assist when problems arise. Use multiple means of keeping people on top of things: memos, meetings, discussion groups, and especially getting out there and talking to your people.

Talk up the change, your vision through the change, and plans, strategies, and goals. Keep it going. Once at the beginning will not nearly be enough. This has to be something that becomes part of your daily sound bytes.

Make sure everyone knows what is most important, i.e. what you are about (who you are and what is important to you): your beliefs about work, your values, and the qualities that are most important to you.

Don't forget about working to get them on board the problems, the solutions, and the final outcomes. If they are vested in what is happening, they will help make a difference.

Have you had problems communicating with your boss, a difficult employee, or another colleague?

> Open the doors with your positivity. Be patient. Keep at it. You have lost the war if you can't communicate – there are always (Yes, ALWAYS!) ways to improve communications with someone.
>
> Key idea: any sense of negativity on your part will block success. There are also always ways to communicate

positively. (See also our many specific titles available at www.difficultpeople.org.)

Care

However it is comfortable for you and them, let them know that you care about how this change will affect them individually and as a team.

Take care of yourself and make sure your team members are taking care of themselves (see Chapters 22 and 23).

Acknowledgment, recognition, reward and celebration

Forget something? Far too many managers do. What may seem like the most insignificant change to you may have a marked impact on others. When we acknowledge people; personnel transitions will go considerably more smoothly. Letting things take their course, may work in the long run, but people will enjoy work a whole lot more and people will accept changes, especially personnel changes, more readily if we spend that little bit of extra time paying attention to how they are 'getting on.' Throwing in a few compliments doesn't hurt either.

Deal with things NOW!

As if you have the time. Right?!

Time management is, of course, a major issue for managers (see Chapter 19) but it is not an acceptable excuse when it comes to spending time with your people. If it is going to affect someone, get it done. Put those other things on the back burner and address the issues that are impacting how your team members are feeling and thinking, because if you don't, I guarantee you will have significantly more time management issues down the road.

Get creative

When you run into road blocks, do something! Get people involved in the challenge presented by the concern and in finding solutions. Take intelligent, calculated chances if you need to. I have rarely seen a problem that a bunch of people couldn't solve.

Motivation

You don't have to be a great motivational speaker, you have to be you and you have to be willing to let people know who that 'you' is. Is the persona you want your team members to believe in a stick-to-the-desk, nose-to-the-grindstone, workaholic, or is it a bit of that and a whole lot more? People are motivated primarily by what they see you do, and by what you say; and especially when they see you live what you say.

Time

Be patient. As much as you would like to charge ahead and get through this whole change process and reap the benefits of 'being there,' it takes time for people to adjust. It takes time even if you do everything listed above right. (Hopefully, it takes less time, but it still takes time.)

Remember Self-Worth

All change affects people's sense of self. Difficulties throughout the change process will affect how your people feel about themselves. Keep in mind that whatever you do or propose to do, change will make a difference and people will look to you for support and stability throughout this process.

This is especially true if someone feels they have been victimized, taken advantage of, if they are resentful about something, and if they feel vulnerable (a very common reaction during change). You can make a big difference to how they feel and how they react simply by paying positive attention to them. It doesn't have to take a lot of time out of your schedule. Often a quick phone call, or better yet, a personal stop-by, raises the level exponentially.

> I remember an incident when I was the newly appointed Administrative Dean of a summer program. For several weeks I went about my duties as competently as I could hoping I was doing what I had been hired to do. Nary a word from the camp director, pro or con, about my efforts that whole time, though we interacted several times a day. Finally after what seemed like a long period of time, just in passing, he said something about how he appreciated my hard work. Even though I hadn't realized how much the tension had been building, I understood it at that

moment. It was like a flood of stress washed out of me. I was a whole lot more positive and confident about what I was doing after that, and I bet other people noticed, too.

It is often those little moments that make so much difference to people. And we let so many of them get by. Remind yourself daily that you can make a difference in small and BIG ways.

Questions and Ideas for Contemplation

The changes referred to in this chapter are perhaps the most significant to you in your role as a middle manager and leader because you are intimately involved in almost everything that happens and with everyone who is affected by the change. You can also be involved in, and have an impact on, much of what happens as a result of these types of changes.

In the next chapter we will discuss more 'monumental' business-wide changes, and you certainly can have a positive impact for your team in working with and through those changes as well, but part of those types of changes are far beyond your control or influence.

See Chapter 22 for a brief look at the impact of change and ideas for dealing with it when a new leader takes the helm of a team.

Chapter 16

Big Changes Matter Too

Major change, typically instigated high up the corporate ladder, has a marked impact on the entire organization:

Mergers

Acquisitions

Restructuring, caused by many factors

Bankruptcy or other financial difficulties

New CEO, and/or other top managers are replaced

Adjustments because of competition, productivity needs, etc.

While the causes may be varied, the effect on managers and personnel up and down the chain can be tremendous and even horrendous: people lose jobs, are relocated, moved to new divisions or onto different teams; they may have to adjust to new management and management styles; there can be cultural changes; budgets may change dramatically; whole divisions and locations may disappear with the resultant loss of jobs or 'forced' relocation – in short, **people** are affected.

It may very well seem to the personnel and managers in the trenches that the corporate bigwigs could care less about how they are impacted. It often feels like the true onus of dealing with the many adjustments falls squarely on the shoulders of mid-level management. It takes quality leadership to keep one's head above water and one's team moving in a positive direction. In this Chapter we will discuss some of the challenges that must be dealt with as the result of corporate-wide changes.

Your Focus

As a leader your primary concern comes back to your team and your people. When you are able to focus on what is best for you and them, you stand a chance of making it through the quagmire of what is usually a long and difficult transition process.

I have witnessed and been involved in a number of major corporate-level 'restructurings' caused by a number of factors (acquisition, restructuring due to personnel loss or changes, etc.). Even in the cases where upper level management made an effort to make the transition process as smooth as possible, the changes hit people very hard in many cases, and affected everyone involved in many ways. Adjustments took long periods of time, i.e. months and years.

Take Care of Your People

Typically there is a great deal of uncertainty, confusion, and trepidation following these types of major change. People will often be in shock. Everyone will be asking, "What does this mean to me and my family." Later on they will also think, "What does this mean for our team."

Initially your job as leader is to provide a foundation of support. That is first and foremost probably more intangible than tangible support. In spite of what you may be going through yourself you have to reflect a calm, in-control persona. You need to be able to let everyone know that you are on top of things as much as you can be and that you will make every effort to keep them informed at every turn. Create an aura where they understand that whatever may happen, you are not going to leave them hanging or outside the loop.

You also need to let them know exactly what you can and can't do for them. This is no place for pie-in-the-sky predictions or claims. Generally speaking you won't know much more than they do, but showing them that you are maintaining control and letting them know you will keep them posted goes a long way to easing the initial shock and panic.

Prepare

You can also help people prepare for what may come. If your company has been taken over by another, there are many possibilities of what might happen to you and others. Wise leaders make sure people get proactive in taking care of themselves and the team. You can provide encouragement and support in helping people consider options, prepare materials, make contacts, etc. In many large corporate-led changes, you will also be able to offer them a wide range of services provided through Human Resources or other departments (legal, financial, benefits, etc.).

Again, it is important to get people moving. Once they start taking some kind of action, even if at this early stage it is a shot in the dark, they are getting some of their control back and as a result their self-confidence and self-worth.

Specific recommendations

Here is a short list of things managers can help personnel consider:

> Getting resumes in order

> Contacting and talking to recruiters

> Recommend (or even purchase and disperse) books, materials, courses on change and loss

> Provide or recommend coaching or counseling services [sometimes offered or available in-house, sometimes can be budgeted]

>> FACT! It is amazing how much funding for a wide variety of services and products is available if you are willing to look for it. Many, if not most, major corporations have pools of money set aside for special purposes OR if you are willing to stick your neck out just a little bit and ask, there are ways to inquire about or apply for funding for special purposes: seminars, workshops, and trainings; coaching; counseling; educational and motivational materials; and so on. I have found funding for special projects and ideas in the oddest places, but you do have to seek and be willing to ask.

> Keep everyone up to date on services offered in house relevant to the transition

>> Organize or recommend meetings to discuss options, concerns, problems personnel are encountering

Share information across the group: formally in meetings or informally as a means of keeping team spirit and effort focused on helping each other

Coordinate efforts across the group (for just about anything) to help everyone stay involved, focused, and working as a team

Help people stay focused on team vision, quality, and their work. This can help ease a good bit of stress while everyone is waiting for 'what comes next.'

Phase II

Businesses love to label things, so I'm taking this terminology from a transition (acquisition) I witnessed. Phase II is the 'when things really start happening phase,' which in reality means, we finally know at least something about what is happening or what is going to happen to ourselves, our team, and our personnel.

If you have gotten through 'Phase I' successfully and managed to keep everyone moving in a positive direction, this phase can be somewhat more bearable in spite of what may come down the pike. And what comes down the pike can be very traumatic: people may very well lose jobs or have to relocate if they want to keep their jobs; teams may be disrupted by incoming personnel and/or loss of personnel; new management may be brought in; 'The way we have always done things around here,' may change dramatically; and so on.

Recommendations for Phase II

Stick with everything that is working in the above recommendations for 'Phase I'.

Stay in contact with your people. This is when they need your leadership the most. Lead – not from your office on your butt, but out there where they are. It will be good for them and for you.

Information sharing is one of your greatest tools. People want to know what is happening. They will appreciate anything you can tell them.

Let and get people talking. Rumors will fly, people will speculate, and none of that is necessarily bad, because talking things out is generally good. However, if someone is consistently spreading erroneous information or doom and gloom without any foundation in reality, that needs to be nipped in the bud, and quickly.

Help people handle individual concerns as they arise and as you can. Your role as mentor and advisor takes on a new meaning when someone is being let go, or reassigned.

Stay on top of how people feel. Professional help may be warranted if someone is unable to handle the stresses and difficulties they face.

Establish and maintain communications with as many departments, divisions, and upper-level managers as you can. The more information you have the better you can help your personnel.

Always maintain a focus on the values and qualities that have made a difference for you and for your team. Quality matters, even in difficult times.

Take care of yourself and your family. You are not going to be of much help to others if you are over-stressed or ill. When things seem overwhelming find support: from colleagues, from your family, get a coach, etc. (See Chapter 23)

The Worst Case Scenario

Take your pick: your entire team is out of a job; you get a new boss whose personality is akin to a grizzly bear; you have to relocate 2000 miles if you want to keep your job; your team is being broken into five different groups and you are losing most of your key personnel while having to assimilate new personnel from other locations; i.e. write your own dismal scenario...

The best leaders help their personnel up to the time they walk out the door. There are a thousand-thousand things to think about, prepare for, and do, but the most important is to take care of yourself and your players, 'your people.' Help people do what they need to do.

You can help them through support, by keeping them focused and proactive, by offering ideas and suggestions, by helping them with closure for this time and part of their life, in short, by being there, by understanding, by caring.

Questions and Ideas for Contemplation

The most significant thing people will remember about having lived through a major disruption at work is <u>how they were treated</u>. You can't speak to or take on the responsibility for how corporate treats them, but you can respect them, understand, and care. It may (will likely) make the transition considerably easier for them and they are more likely to tackle whatever follows with a positive conviction and a commitment to excellence.

See Chapter 23, "Dealing with Major Corporate Change: An Acquisition" for a brief overview of how you can approach this type of major corporate change.

Chapter 17

Open Communications

Most managers know how important communications are. What they don't seem to understand is how much better their communications could and should be. It is so much easier to get by with how we normally are and how we normally do things, than to put the time and effort into working on our interactions with others.

We would be better leaders if we did.

Most Important Point

Whether we run a ten person team or a two hundred person division, most of us don't get out amongst our people anywhere near enough. Tom Peters has been shouting this from the rooftops in his books for years. Many other business authors also consider this a key idea. So why don't we listen?

We All have Good Excuses

I have heard every excuse there is to why this simple but seemingly hard to implement concept gets shuffled to the side. Most of the time it boils down to time management (See Chapter 19) and priorities.

Here are a couple of very good ideas that dovetail each other – you really should only have these two essential priorities at work:

> What your team and organizational vision focus on

> Your people

If it isn't related to either one of these, it is second string. If you are giving away your time to other issues that aren't first string, you are short changing yourself, your people, your team, and your organization. Period. (Go ahead and shout some more Tom.)

When you retire, do you want excuses to be the foundation for why you didn't give your people the time they needed?

There are NO good excuses for the rest of your life.

Sorry to belabor this point, but...

GET OUT THERE AND TALK TO YOUR PEOPLE
ON THEIR TURF!

It has all been Said Before

Much of what I have written in this book is about communications. I have also emphasized communication skills and techniques in all of my writings about "Understanding and Working with Difficult People." (Slogan of difficultpeople.org) Below are some highlighted items that can further help you as you lead others through change and difficulties.

It is no Time for being Cute

Change is tough on people. Direct, open, forthright communications are an absolute necessity from my point of view. Throw out the subtle tactics until things settle down a bit. Keep it simple, keep it coming, and don't mince words. You may find it works amazingly well with people. So well, you won't play so many games in the future.

Listening

These next ideas come from our books *Understanding and Working with Difficult People* and *Me! A Difficult Person?* These are great communication tools and skills that you can develop if you pay attention and practice.

Perceptions are everything

Literally! What you mean has no bearing on an interaction unless you can get that meaning across. Pay attention to what you say and how you say it. Pay attention to how the other person receives it and ask if you have any doubt about their understanding, or yours.

Listening actively

Many difficult people are acting difficult simply because they do not FEEL they are being heard, accepted, that they belong, and/or that their intent is getting fulfilled. By listening carefully, attentively, and actively you can often defuse a difficult situation and quite possibly have the person come to respect you because you have made the effort. Almost always with respect comes a change in difficult behavior.

Most of us know that listening carefully, hearing what a person is saying, is an important part of good communication. When working with people in difficult situations, you not only need to listen carefully, you need to **let them know** you are listening to them carefully, that **they have been heard**, and that **you understand** what they are saying!

Give them a chance to talk without interruption. This often takes patience. Try to erase any preconceptions you have about them or what they are going to say, even if they are upset. Your calm self-confidence will help keep the situation under control and certainly will help defuse a situation that is out-of-control. Your willingness to let them speak first, and freely, shows respect for them. They will appreciate it.

Part of listening is feedback via non-verbal communications and simple 'yeses,' 'uh-huhs,' 'nods,' etc. In difficult situations you want to go beyond these important forms of feedback by being more definitive, "I hear what you are telling me," "I understand," etc.

You want to go beyond this by repeating back what they are telling you, "backtracking." When you repeat an important phrase, idea, bit of information, back to a person, it tells them beyond any doubt that you have heard what they have said. It is possible to go overboard with this, but most of us don't do it enough.

One of the keys to backtracking is to focus on important information or ideas they are saying and give them feedback on key points. Backtracking in this way is a form of acknowledgment and can be perceived as a form of recognition.

Understanding

> "...difficult people become even more difficult
>
> when they are misunderstood"
>
> (Bell and Smith)

"or perceive to be misunderstood."

(Koob)

Backtracking can also denote understanding and gives you the opportunity to seek clarity as well.

"What I'm hearing you say is..."

"Does this mean that x and y are part of this?"

Asking clarifying questions is a very useful tool for you to further understand something that is not clear, and an excellent way to let them know you are interested and <u>want</u> to understand.

Feelings

Understanding the person's feelings, especially during times of crises, and making an effort to acknowledge their feelings are also key tools in communicating.

Say it!

"I understand that you are very upset about this. Let's talk some about how this restructuring is affecting you."

Do it with compassion and kindness.

Asking questions – a tool managers could use much more, especially in difficult times.

It shows a desire to understand.

Use open-ended questions that begin with, **"how, what, when, who, where"**; avoid using "why"–it is accusatory. Also, try to avoid using the word "**but**," it qualifies and diminishes what they are telling you.

"Why do you want to do it this way?"

Often this type of question will be interpreted by another person as a type of 'attack'. Especially if the inflection, tone, body language, word emphasis add to the mix:

"Why do you want to do it **this** way?"

Better:

"John, what you have said is very interesting. I'd like to know more about how you see this working. It is different from what I was thinking, so it would be helpful to understand where you want to go with this. Can you give me a more in-depth understanding?"

There are always less-charged, kinder ways to say and ask things if we watch our communication patterns and make the effort!

Take notes?

This may seem odd in the middle of a difficult situation, but a simple statement like, "Hold on one second, this is important to you and I want to make sure I get it right," can show someone you are serious about helping. They will know that you are serious when you pull out a notebook and take notes on key points.

Seek specificity

The more you know the better and your interest in seeking clarity and increased understanding will often be appreciated more than you will know. It helps denote the desire to understand and it makes people feel like they and what they are concerned with matters. When you have doubts, when you are still not sure what they are feeling, thinking or what is happening, ask, ask, ask – ask kindly.

Bring it all together

Summarizing at the end of a conversation also shows understanding and interest. It lets the other person know you have been listening carefully and that you got their intent. If there are any questions on your part or they still seem hesitant, then ask them if you got it right.

Thank them

The simplest communication tool of them all, but too often left out. Thank them for their input, their honesty, their willingness to share. Thank them in some way. This shows compassion, caring, and a willingness to make a difference.

Important

Don't expect them to come to you with their concerns. Go to them. Don't expect them to necessarily open up right away or be able to communicate clearly and concisely what they are concerned about. Part of your task as a leader is to draw them out. Through your integrity and concern you establish the trust that helps open the doors of communication a bit wider each time you interact with them.

It is often about Information

Just to belabor this point once more – not knowing something is very frustrating and very damaging to people's self-worth. Difficult times call for extraordinary measures. Share everything you can and let them know what you don't know or what you are not at liberty to share. It makes a BIG difference in how people handle change and handle processing through change.

Questions and Ideas for Contemplation

Have I said enough? Perhaps too much in one sense, and not enough in another. You, as a leader, are wise enough to translate this into positive action. Think your communications style and techniques through thoroughly. Make a concerted effort to change the things that will help make a difference when you are leading others through difficult situations.

Chapter 18

Barriers to Better Communications

From my humble perspective there are two very common and primary reasons people have difficulties communicating, both are rooted in the same cause.

The Problems

> Need to be Right.
>
> Reluctance (Fear) of communicating

The Cause

Poor Self-Worth, which often translates to replacing our poor self-value with ego.

Ego

There is a lot of it going around – much more than we would think or be willing to admit. Our ego is much more than 'being egotistical.' Ego means that our self-worth is low, we lack confidence, and we lack self-control – we replace it with: worry, blame, complaining, defensiveness, and raising ourselves above others (often in very subtle ways that are very difficult to recognize).

Consider the following:

> If we are being defensive/reacting negatively to someone, we are 'in ego' and not 'in self-worth.' We lose control, and instead of responding from a calm, self-controlled stance we react in some negative way.
>
> When we worry, we are placing control outside our self to 'what might happen,' or 'what someone might do.'
>
> When we blame and complain, we are not taking ownership of our life and work, but placing that

responsibility on others. Important: It doesn't matter if we are 'right' or not.

When we are afraid or fearful of some problem or potential outcome we lack self-confidence and we give our power over to the negative situation.

The Need to be Right

Ego wants us to be right. The key point is that much of our communication difficulties with other people come from both parties needing to be right. When you (or both of you) can step back from being right and make other choices, the communication concerns disappear.

By far the majority of the time we don't NEED to be right. As a leader there are better ways to communicate what needs to be done and what we want to get across, without forcing people to accept something. Even on the rare occasions when we need to be right, there are kinder, more gentler ways of saying and doing things.

One of the best ways to avoid communications conflicts with people who need to be right is to observe your own communications and to ask yourself, "Do I need to be right in this circumstance or is there a way for them to be right and for us to accomplish what we need to accomplish?" Leaders who have a strong sense of self-worth do not need to be right. They do need to get things done and get things done well, but that is a whole different ball game from 'being right.'

> Once when I was giving a motivational seminar a member of an audience asked me whether it was possible to be right and to be kind at the same time. I thought for a moment and said, "Yes, there are always ways to say something more kindly." Later that evening I thought about that question and my answer, and I knew that I had only half-answered the question. What I should have included in my answer was, "What is so all-fired important about being right?"

Most of the time, we can give up being right. It comes from our ego – our need to bolster our self with others. The next time you are having a difficult conversation with a 'difficult person,' try to see whether some or all of the conflict comes from either or both of you needing to 'be right.' Then see what it takes to step back from your position and take another tack. The first few times it won't be easy because we REALLY don't want to give up being right. Try it once, you will see. We really, really, really, don't want to give up being right.

Guess what? Neither do they.

"If you have a choice between being right and being kind, choose being kind."

Wayne Dyer

Fear in Communications

Some people just don't communicate well. They seem to hold everything inside, refuse to respond, or they run around in circles without ever really saying anything definitive or of substance. Their lack of self-worth and self-confidence are affecting their ability to communicate effectively. They are afraid to make mistakes or feel they may sound inept.

The 'cure' is patience, coupled with encouragement and support. This is very hard to do because we typically don't feel we have the time to waste to dealing with a person whose communications are frustrating to us. But the payoff may very well be an employee who contributes a great deal more to your team and the organization. It is important to remember, however, that any sign of frustration or negativity will send them back into their hiding place.

Take it slow, do it over a longer period of time, and give them a chance to feel comfortable and to open up. You can even talk to them about their communications and how you would like them to feel more comfortable with you and what you will do for them. Help them to be right. Offer them positive feedback when they come through.

You lead

Good communications often come from our ability to communicate well with a given person by keenly observing what we are saying and how it impacts them. Often we can turn difficult situations into much more positive interactions by keeping our ego out of the mix and working to keep the lines open through our own personal skills.

Questions and Ideas for Contemplation

Every challenging communication situation is different, see how you can make adjustments in order to facilitate what is happening between you and the other person. After a little practice you will find you naturally start watching what and how you say things and you will find you have far fewer communication problems and obstacles than you used to.

Chapter 19

Time Management

A truncated dissertation on time management tools and skills

OR

A brief philosophical inquiry into time management

It is Your Problem; Not 'Theirs'

Believe it or not YOU cause your own time management concerns!

I have heard every excuse in the book and I have seen many managers point their fingers to something or someone other than themselves:

> "My boss, job, people, (fill-in-the-blank), demand too much of me"
>
> "I have too many meetings"
>
> "Human Resources keeps coming down with all these programs we have to take"
>
> "There is just too much to do"
>
> "I'm handling two jobs, here."
>
> and so on

Take Responsibility!

The biggest problem to better time management is that most of us think we are doing the best we can under the circumstances. The truth is, most of us **can do better.** We can all learn to practice better time management.

The biggest obstacle to being a successful time manager is:

Admitting and accepting that you <u>can</u> do better.

It doesn't hurt to admit you can use some help learning better time management skills, as well.

> I know that it isn't easy to accept that we aren't the best we can be at something and we all want to feel like we are doing a pretty good job at managing our time. However, you can probably look back at many aspects of your life to this point and realize that you have learned a great deal and become much more skilled at doing things that you used to think you were good at.

Time management is something we can always improve:

> Partially because there are new skills we can learn

> And partly because there is slippage, i.e. we forget to use some of the techniques and skills we already know and we fall back into old habits.

Hey some Seminars ARE Useful.

The best time management seminars I am aware of have managers do an exercise right from the get-go.

The gist of the exercise is simple: map out a week, or better yet a month, in great detail, of how you spend (or recently spent) your time.

It is an eye opening exercise for almost everyone. It is an exercise that, if you have time management concerns, you should do right now. The key is to be thorough and absolutely honest.

You will find out a number of useful things:

> What you actually do spend your time on – most people are very surprised when they see their typical week laid out in a broad chart that delineates specifically what they spend their time on.

> You can also single out the different areas you spend the most time on. This adds even more value to the exercise.

> [I recommend using different colored magic markers to high-light each significant area in your schedule: one-on-ones; group meetings; e-mail time; phone time; etc. Then you will have a perspective that allows you to immediately recognize those areas that take up significant

amounts of your time.]

It will tell you, with no hidden agenda, what your priorities are – what you are spending the most time on. [If what you discover really are not your priorities, then you have some adjusting to do.]

It will tell you what other people are seeing you spend your time on. If you are not spending it on them, they will know, and now you do too. If you are not spending it on your own priorities, the things that you claim to be most important, they will know that too.

Your use of time speaks volumes about what is important to you as a manager and leader. Choose wisely.

The learning keeps coming, study that chart you just made!

Priorities

I stated this previously, but it is worth reiterating here from a slightly different perspective:

If you have a clear and impelling vision for your team that meshes with the corporate or organizational vision (and it should), that is one of your top priorities:

Anything that <u>directly</u> affects or impacts your vision

(values, goals, mission)

is a top priority.

The key word here is DIRECTLY.

Your other top priority is:

Your people

If these two areas are getting short-changed because of secondary or tertiary meetings, memos, phone calls, redundant programs, or whatever is taking up a lot of your time, you are wasting time on things that can wait.

I am so adamant about this that I believe we should make it very clear as a manager what our priorities are, what we intend to spend our time on, and make that patently obvious to everyone up, down, and sideways in the chain. Then we need to live it.

If you do this, believe it or not within a very short period of time, other people will begin to make an effort not to waste your time. You do this by letting them know what you are willing to spend time on – what is really important.

Yes, sometimes you have to take a bit of a risk or make some hard choices, but it is either that or, well, have time management problems. The interesting part of this is that if (and when) you let people know that you can't come to their meeting, or do 'X' **because you have to spend time on the quality, values, mission, and people that make a difference**, they will understand. You might even rub off on a few of them and get them pointed in the right direction too.

In my mind every other time management idea is secondary to this key point. I am going to list a few great tools and ideas below, but these are simply things you can do to save time here or there. The real time savings is when you decide to follow your priorities.

Miscellaneous favorite time management ideas

What is Sacred?

I love bringing this up in a seminar. Is there anything sacred about a half hour or an hour? What is wrong with a twenty minute meeting? If you have all your ducks in a row, I will bet you can get through most half hour meetings in twenty minutes, hour meetings in forty, etc.

Once you buy into this idea, you can run with it. It does work!

The next time someone calls and asks if you could meet with them for an hour, tell them you have twenty-two and a half minutes available at four-forty-three. You will probably get a long silence on the other end of the line, and then perhaps a chuckle. But you will also have set the stage for letting them know what time you actually can afford. If you do set up a meeting with them, then stick to the time schedule you set. Not only does this set a precedent, it is fun. You will have them wondering for days!

It is all about Organization (and having some guts)

Meetings could be half as long or less if:

You make sure you have a detailed agenda.

You have everything prepared ahead of time: slide decks, notes, materials, etc. Anything anyone else needs to see before hand should be sent in plenty of time.

Stick to the agenda and to your time schedule. If you are leading a meeting, you can learn to keep things focused and on track. Don't let egotists hog the floor for long periods of time or let people argue about relatively irrelevant points forever.

Ask this question to yourself, frequently, and out loud when appropriate:

"What does this have to do with our priorities?" (Vision, values, qualities, people)

You insist that everyone read/look at appropriate materials (slide decks, notes, agenda) ahead of time. Remind them ahead of time that you expect them to come prepared. Which means that if they don't come prepared, you have the right (actually it is imperative) to ignore their inquiries and move ahead. They will get the message really fast, if you stick to your guns.

As a manager you sometimes have to let people know what you expect:

"I'm sorry Steve, but we need to move ahead here. The data you are asking to see are in the materials I sent you on Tuesday. Please, everyone, be sure to review everything we send carefully before attending meetings."

You don't have to be nasty, but you may have to be frank, especially if this behavior has been the norm. Set precedents, let people know what they are, and then stick to them!

It is all about Sticking to Your Guns (and Time Schedule)

See above and...don't let people take up your time unless this is 'people time' for you.

> There was another graduate student who came into the Doctoral program at the University of Illinois the same summer as I did. He had credentials out the wazoo, was extremely intelligent, but he couldn't stop talking. He would corner anyone he could and yammer away forever (if you let him). We all quickly learned to escape his clutches ASAP. He flunked out at the end of that summer. He never got anything done. If we had listened to him, we wouldn't have either.

When you gotta go. Go!

If you are in the middle of a meeting that is scheduled to end at four and your walking around time starts at four, leave. Whoever is running that meeting should have learned what you have already learned – you stick to your meeting times and schedule!

You will have to decide if you can do this if it is your boss running the meeting, but I typically never played any favorites even when it came to bosses. Just be judicious and think of a great reason why you have to go! Or, better yet, let them know ahead of time that you have to leave at 4:00 P.M. on the nose.

There is another hint in this about priorities – your walking around time is a number one priority. Is this meeting? If you choose to stay, you are saying something about just how important your people really are. Remember, they will notice.

Don't be afraid to raise your hand

I learned a long time ago that meetings quickly get out of hand and out of time if the meeting's leader doesn't control things. I also learned to get people back on track even when I am not leading a meeting because I HATE TO WASTE TIME, especially my own. Raise your hand a lot!

> Hint: This actually works!

Raise your hand and don't be afraid to say, "I think we have talked this out and seem to be running in circles. Let's vote and see where we stand on this. (This was my favorite tactic. I instigated lots of votes.) Or, you could say,

> "We are getting way off base here, John (meeting moderator) could you refocus us?"

Yes, you might get a 'reputation,' but ninety percent of the people will thank you when they get to go home earlier from that four P.M. meeting that actually DID end on time at five.

Those wonderful Little Blocks of Time

My favorite time management tool is using all those little blocks of wasted time we have during the day. And yes, you very likely do have them!

If you think you don't have any of these, try paying attention to how you spend all of your time. Typically there are many moments in a day that we can use if we decide to make use of them and are prepared to do so:

> Waiting for someone to answer the phone or get back to you when they are called away or waiting for someone to actually answer the phone when you are on hold by some 'system.' (You can look through ten or more memos or e-mails in that time!)

> Walking from here to there – Of course, we now have cell phones and PDAs, but if you don't have anyone to call, there are many other things you can accomplish you if you remember to bring what you need along. [I often carry papers, books, and/or a notebook with me on my many jaunts.]

> Waiting for meetings to start or to end, so you can enter the room – typically you can get a lot done at these times.

> Standing in line in the cafeteria, bank, check out, etc

> Walking from there to here – most of us tend to do a LOT of walking in a day.

While I was a graduate student, I used to get ninety percent of my studying done walking around, standing in line, or waiting for something. Today I do ninety percent of my research reading for my books the same way. (And that IS the truth! Of course, I do find lots of excuses to do a good bit of walking from here to there and there to here!)

Delegate? Who said Delegate?

What is it about managers that they can't seem to trust someone else to handle a variety of tasks for them, or go to a meeting and report results, or review an article, etc., etc.?

The best managers, LEADERS, I know latch onto their best people immediately and give them responsibility. And they do the same with everyone else, especially the underachievers because it is one of the best ways to help them assume more responsibility and to train them. Yes, you do have to pay some attention to them initially, but most of them will blossom. If you are willing to give them a chance and it will pay huge dividends in your time management concerns.

No? I really meant, "Yes."

Managers on the way up often have trouble saying, "No." They especially have trouble saying, "No!" And it is highly unlikely that they would ever say, **"NO!"** So everyone quickly learns they actually mean, "Yes!"

Actually I meant, "No."

And I mean, **NO!** Really.

It is unlikely that you are going to jeopardize your career by occasionally saying, "No," even to those above you or lateral to you in the chain. You are more likely to jeopardize your career and leadership capabilities if you are ignoring your priorities because you can't say, 'No,' and mean it, as you will end up with far too much on your plate.

How DO you say 'No?'

How do you say, 'No,' without causing upset or perturbation?

Tell the truth, kindly:

> "Ruth, I know this is important to you, but I am completely booked, and I really can't do this for you. I know Dave has expressed an interest in this project, why don't you see if the two of you could collaborate? Plus, I know he wants more experience in this area."

> "Jeff, I would love to help old buddy, but I already have

too much on my plate. If you want me to review what you put together, I will be happy to once it is done. I know you will do a great job."

Yes, people may be disappointed a bit at first that you aren't willing to cave in to all their wishes anymore, but if you want to build the best team possible and maintain your own sanity as well, be willing to express, kindly, what you need to stay on top of your own business at hand.

What do I do with all the Time I Save?

Do you know what most people do with all that 'extra' time when they have finally cut their work week down to only fifty hours at the office and a 'few more' hours catching up at home?

They fill it up with more work.

If you want to delve into the psychology behind this, you would probably find out that besides the fear of failure or measuring up, people are afraid not to be doing something. We are **used to** working all the time.

Do we ever learn?

Not unless we make the effort.

Work is a habit.

Overwork is a habit, too.

I recommend taking a few deep breaths once in awhile and at the very least spending a few minutes contemplating what you might do with the time you have saved.

You will be glad you did. Your family will be glad you did. You will probably find that your employees, coworkers, and bosses will be glad you did, too.

Now...

...you will have more time to manage change!

Questions and Ideas for Contemplation

There is a good bit more I could say, but then that would take up too much of your time. However, this stuff IS worth thinking about. Most importantly, be willing to consider the possibility that **you** actually **can make a difference** to your overworked schedule.

YOU are the key to successful time management.

Chapter 20

Bringing in the Cavalry

A wise leader uses every resource at her disposal in helping her team deal with change. Often large corporations have extant programs available or create specialized seminars and trainings during times of major transitions. Outsourcing may also be a choice if resources are available locally. Consider all the possibilities. The more informed you and your team members are the better they will be able to handle the pressures caused by major change and/or ongoing change.

Choices

The following is a list of resources that might be helpful and available for individuals and teams as they work through the change process.

Materials directly related to the impact of change, dealing with change, loss, and grieving

> Books and other written materials

> Web materials, web sites (e.g. www.difficultpeople.org provides books, and other materials centered around, "Understanding and Working with Difficult People and in with Difficult Situations")

> Tapes or DVDs and other audio/visual materials

Seminars, Workshops, Trainings on a wide variety of topics (see below)

> Corporate provided

> > Available through company web network

Human Resource programs

Legal advice

Financial programs

Relocation programs

Outsourcing

Coaches*

Counselors**

Motivational speakers

Business group seminars

Financial experts

Legal advise

Relocation

*Coaches – coaches support clients through change and the difficulties engendered by change and loss. They are very effective in helping people see the range of choices they have. Many coaches also provide support and informational seminars and workshops. Coaches may be available in house through Human Resources or other departments or hired independently

Personal/Life coaches

Executive, Managerial

Dealing with difficult people

Dealing with difficult situations

Dealing with change and loss

Financial coaches

Etc.

[Visit http://www.difficultpeople.org. Dr. Koob and our other coaches work in these and other specialty areas.]

**Counselors – Can also be very helpful during initial change crises and throughout the change process for those who are having difficulty with stress and other concerns. They may be available in house through Human Resources or other departments.

Topics for seminars, workshops, presentations, coaching

The best coaches and seminar leaders who give these types of workshops design them around your needs and concerns. Seminars and workshops can range from several hours to full day off-sites.

The Impact of Change – this is a very valuable training seminar that can help prepare/provide information about the many issues related to how change may impact your team members and your team/organization

The Change Process – takes the 'Impact of Change' a step further and considers how change affects us throughout the change process and key ideas for dealing with change

Dealing with Change – in-depth seminar on skills and tools to help everyone in your group manage change

Dealing with Difficult Situations – workshop designed to address specific change issues related to your group. Coaches or seminar leaders with a general knowledge of your business and who have the ability to design a workshop specifically related to your concerns are optimal.

Dealing with Difficult People – Change and Loss tend to bring out the best and worst in people. Problems can become exacerbated because of the stress and control issues engendered by change. Some coaches are specialists in this area

Leaders Managing Change – focuses on key issues for leaders. This can be designed for specific emphasis or a more broad approach focusing on information, skills, and tools (as discussed in this book). Exercises tailored for your group needs can be developed.

Dealing with Resistance – This is a seminar for managers and key personnel in helping deal with the difficulties that arise when people create significant obstacles to moving through the change process successfully.

Dealing with Loss – considers the difficulties people encounter when loss of job, relocation, or other losses are a significant part of the change process

Processing Grief – 'Stages' or 'Symptoms" (Anger, stress, depression, etc.) of the grieving process engendered by loss. These may also be discussed in a "Dealing with Loss" seminar

Dealing with Non-stop/Continuous Change – Considers the specific issues, skills, and tools, managers and teams need to deal with the constant change prevalent in our current global business environment

Team Building through Change – information, exercises, skills, and tools managers and teams can use to build or maintain their focus, quality, productivity, etc. throughout the change process

Retention during Change – Key ideas for managers relative to the loss of quality personnel during major change

Recruitment issues during/following change – Key ideas for managers who need to fill positions while dealing with change

Time Management – Change often engenders a lot more work for everyone, especially during the early stages when people are confused and stressed. A time management seminar may be just the thing to help them get grounded and in control, even if they have heard most of it before.

And many other business specific seminars – Contact: Human Resources; Legal, Financial, and Relocation Teams/specialists; and Coaches and Consultants who specialize in specific areas you feel could be helpful to your team. High quality seminar leaders will make every effort to design a workshop that is specific to your needs and concerns. [Contact us at http://www.difficultpeople.org or 1 800 928 8735. We offer a wide range of business seminars.]

Make Wise Choices for Your People

Most leaders can find the resources they need to support their personnel if they make the effort. The bottom line is people are hurting during change. They can use all the help they can get and though you are out there and doing everything you can, there are others who can add tremendously to what you can do. This will alleviate some of the pressure on your back and it will also be a great learning tool.

I have never met a seminar I didn't learn something from!

Addendum

Managers and leaders are often reluctant to garner outside assistance. Both men and women leaders seem to have an underlying attitude that it might be construed as a weakness (by employees, coworkers, bosses, etc.). The truth is, it is smart leadership.

Coaches, the 'new' professionals for business leaders, are specifically trained and experienced in helping managers deal with issues that arise and in providing support. Every CEO, VP, Director, etc. I have coached, and all the managers I know who have worked with a coach, have grown in many, many ways and they all have found the experience profoundly useful to their immediate concerns and to their careers. Coaches can also provide many useful seminars for teams that are dealing with difficult situations and change. The whole profession is geared up for support, encouragement, information sharing, and motivation. Wow!

Questions and Ideas for Contemplation

When I have led teams, my personal slogan has always been, 'use what is out there.' I have always encouraged my team members to seek out and 'go for' any and all trainings and support that are available, and if I felt it was important I would find ways to design or create possibilities for what wasn't readily available. Surprisingly if you do a little digging and are willing to stick your neck out just a bit, there are many resources and funds available. Seek, ask, find it, and/or create it, if necessary. The more help you provide yourself and your team, the more you will likely be successful with moving through difficulties efficaciously.

Chapter 21

Non-Stop Change

Our technologically-based, global economy is in a constant state of flux and development. Simply put, we are dealing with change on a daily basis both in our work and in our lives. This impacts not only large corporate considerations like competition, production costs, work force, customer base, etc., it also reaches down to the team and individual level. Learning as much as we can about change, the process of change, and dealing with difficult situations can help us deal more confidently and flexibly with all that will affect us in the days ahead.

Constant change affects us all

Keep in mind that even minor changes affect us all and there is not only a potential excitement and energy as a result, there is also an underlying instability and angst. We deal with this every day!

Leaders Dealing with Constant Change

Anyone reading this book could easily come up with a half-dozen things that have happened in the past week that impacted their team **that they weren't expecting**. How can we stay on top of everything that comes in on a daily basis, and how can we help our team members deal with their changing situations, as well as with the stressors engendered by these concerns?

> In *Difficult Situations: Dealing with Change* I discuss key ideas in Chapter 26 that help us deal with non-stop change. I will list these key words and phrases below and then add some additional ideas that are particularly relevant to helping others deal with ongoing changes at work.

Stay flexible

When we have the ability to accept what comes at us out of the blue and make adjustments on the spur of the moment, we are much more likely to weather concerns that arise. The ability to be flexible grows from self-worth and self-confidence. (See immediately below and Appendix I, "The Seven Keys to Understanding and Working with Difficult People.")

The Seven Keys to Understanding and Working with Difficult People

Self-awareness

Self-Worth

Self-confidence

Self-control

Honesty

Kindness

Positivity

Creativity

We can react to change creatively – an intelligent and fun way to deal with those things that impact us directly; and we can **be** creative – taking the world by the horns and making it our own. We can also encourage creativity and 'out-of-the-box' thinking in our team members.

Both these are great ways to approach life and business.

Creativity is something leaders should consistently foster, support, and reward in their team members. Some of us are more naturally creative than others, but we can all add to the power and energy of a group by feeling empowered to add our 'two cents' at any time. The best ideas often come to us out-of-the-blue. Make sure everyone on your team feels free to bring those notions forward.

Stay alert

The things that have just 'come my way' at the right time in life have been nothing short of amazing. When I have paid attention, I have managed to learn, grow, and create from these impetuses far more than I would have if I had plodded doggedly ahead through life.

Pay attention to what comes into your life serendipitously.

Be willing to accept difficulties that happen as challenges.

AND

Encourage in your team members a sense of curiosity and

awareness that keeps them open to new ideas

and new ways of doing things.

Serendipity – I sometimes wonder what I have missed because I wasn't paying attention.

Listen

It is not just us listening carefully to others, it is also encouraging everyone to pay attention to everything around them and to develop their listening skills. Good listening skills are certainly helpful in getting ideas across, but the benefits are much greater than that:

Good listening fosters positive information flow (critical to success in all types of change)

Good listening throughout a team supports all team members

Good Listening is a means to very important ends – acknowledgment and attention which help lead to self worth

Good listening fosters learning, ideas, and understanding

Go with the flow

Sometimes we need to bend the rules, kick ourselves into creative gear, and march with a different drummer. At other times it pays to go with the flow of all that is happening and help that flow along as part of your own personal vision and/or the vision of your team. Knowing which is which and when to do one or the other is what paying attention and listening are all about. It is also a key component to leadership.

Make contact, Maintain contact, Communicate, Stay Open to Possibilities

These are points emphasized throughout this book. When you are in touch with your team and each member of your team, you have the capability of responding quickly to concerns and the ability to make a difference NOW! Keeping real lines of communication open throughout your group and throughout the many facets of your organization that you deal with on a daily basis, creates an atmosphere in which people can respond quickly to difficulties that arise, and importantly, helps get the right people on board the problem and solution from the get go.

When you are out there amongst your team members sharing information and keeping your ear to the ground, they are much more likely to follow your lead. Teams that handle change quickly and efficiently do so because they have been taught, primarily through example, how to interact, respond, and make decisions that make a difference.

Be proactive

You can help shape your world!

Be willing to make decisions and take chances

Empower your team members as well. Sudden changes often need quick and decisive actions. When people have the flexibility and freedom to respond intelligently, things get done.

We do shape our world!

Much more than we may think, we shape the world in which we live and work. We always have choices and the choices we make – positive or negative, forward-looking or traditional, flexibly or rigidly – make us who we are and how we impact the world.

Lead and Follow

Keep in mind that everyone approaches things differently. You may have the ideal solution to a problem residing in the mind and skills of a team member who approaches the world and work from a different perspective from yourself. Sometimes the best thing a leader can do for his/her team is to take a step back and let someone else show the way.

It is all about Attitude

Your attitude and approach help to lead others through difficulties. Your integrity, confidence, and self-control say much, much more than anything you put into words. Want to lead well through the ongoing pressures of the dynamic business today?

Then:

> Don't – put on a face of worry, anxiety, blame, complaining, judging, and doom and gloom

> Do – stand tall, be positive, encourage and support others, be open and available, be compassionate and kind, be true to your self

Questions and Ideas for Contemplation

Are you dealing with ongoing change? Take some time to read through "The Seven Keys to Understanding and Working with Difficult People," in Appendix I. See if you can find ways to apply these skills to your own situation. Writing this all out can be very therapeutic.

Chapter 22

Dealing with Leadership Change

A very common type of change that can and often does affect a team dramatically is when a new leader takes the helm. In this brief example you will see how this type of change can impact a group and receive a perspective on how many potential issues can be averted or addressed. Much of what is relevant to this specific type of change could be successfully applied to any type of team change: restructuring, quality improvement strategies, etc.

You have got the Job, Now What?

By far the best thing a new manager can do in helping make his/her transition as a new leader of a team as smooth and concern-free as possible is to get out in the trenches and meet everyone. I am a firm believer in getting to know everyone on my team as soon as possible, and if feasible, learn as much about them even prior to the interview process. The more I know, the better prepared I am, and even more importantly, the more I can relate to them and their concerns.

Team Size

If you are taking over a ten person team, knowing your team players is not as formidable a task as someone who is going to be overseeing five or more smaller teams with a total number of 150 players. Either way, it is important to know as much as possible and to get out and meet everyone. You may need to get creative in how you meet 150 people (small informal get-togethers, wandering through labs or manufacturing, etc.), but it all boils down to making the time, which is a critical element of your early days in a new job.

Before Day 1

If you have accepted a position, you probably know who you are going to be working for and you have a good handle on how many people are on your team and the other line and matrix people you will be in contact with on a regular basis. You may have met some of them through the interview process and if you have done your homework (highly recommended) you have gathered information on your team members and gone through it carefully.

Now get out there ASAP and meet people!

Unfortunately this rarely actually happens in business today. We have orientation, required meetings, etc.

I can't stress this enough: if you haven't met and spoken to everyone on your team and everyone you will have direct contact with throughout your regular work week within ONE week of being on the job, you are not doing your job as a leader of <u>People</u>.

If you do get out there and spend time with everyone – informal, personal time spent in their space (don't have them come to your office for a five minute howdy-do.) – you will very likely have much fewer personnel concerns and transition concerns down the road.

You don't have to spend a great deal of time at this, especially if you are overseeing many smaller teams with lots of players. An informal walk-through with a friendly, firm handshake can do a lot. Learning the names of all those 150+ people leaves a lasting impression, too. Making the effort means a lot to people.

It is a form of acknowledgment.

> For many years I taught large classes at the University level and each semester I would memorize the names of all my 300+ students. They appreciated it, even if I occasionally slipped up, because I made the effort. When I passed them in the street five years later and called them by name, they were even more appreciative of my having remembered them. I quickly got a positive reputation because of the effort I made to do this, even though I tended to be a 'tough' professor.

The point is that even small acknowledgments and brief <u>personal</u> contacts mean a great deal to people.

People appreciate acknowledgment!

Week 1 and Onward

If you have gotten out and about on day one and beyond, keep at it. Make sure you get to everyone.

The next most important thing to do during the first week is to let everyone know **who you are** and **what is important to you**. You can (should!) say this in a formal meeting and you can reiterate it in a formal written statement to your team, but you also have to walk and talk it. Take the opportunity to do this when you are out there talking with everyone. Find the time to slip in a, "I might change a few things around here, but I want you all to know that my focus is on building the best team possible, making sure we are all working well together, and producing the best possible quality." (Or whatever IS important to you.)

Be observant. If you are getting out and about, asking questions, and listening carefully, you will learn a tremendous amount about what your people are all about, who is on top of things and who isn't, where some of the concerns are, where the B.S. is coming from, etc. Managers who sit behind desks reacting to things when they suddenly hit the fan are far behind the eight ball. Getting out and being with your team players, with your colleagues across the chain, and with your boss(es) is about getting to know people, but it is all very much about understanding the dynamics of everything that is going on.

Keep this up: always. There is no end to getting out and being with your team players. There is no end to the support and understanding you can provide, what you can learn and the benefits that come from this practice. As with anything, the tendency is to be gung-ho about this type of technique early on, but to let it slide when things start to pile up. There is very little that is more important than this and if there is, it better be something to do with your highest priorities as set out in your team and organizational visions.

If you are the head of a large team, hopefully the mid-level managers below you will also see the value in this type of regular personal contact with their team players. Make sure you give them the heads up on how important this is and be sure that you encourage, support, and reward appropriate behaviors.

Planning, Strategizing, Making Goals

You may have some great ideas for the team and you may have already formulated some plans and strategies, however, you are going to be far more successful if you broach changes from the standpoint of knowing your people, giving them a chance to tell YOU what needs fixing and what their concerns are, and involving them in the process of making changes. The more input they have, the more likely they will buy into making changes.

Good leaders know how to finesse meetings and conversations so that people consider all the problems and possibilities from every angle possible. Great leaders not only find a way to get their own two cents in and learn about what their team members have to offer, but also learn a great deal about the dynamics of the team. They will garner great ideas from every possible direction as well.

A great tool leaders should use often is: to let others feel they can contribute (or are contributing) to understanding concerns and finding solutions. The more involved people are, the more they own problems and solutions to problems, the easier your managing becomes and the more effective your team will be. This works well at all levels and is even effective up the chain.

> Hint: You are already the boss, you don't need to be 'right' about everything, nor do you need to 'own' everything. Give some things to others and they will often reward you down the road. Plus, you will solve some time management concerns by helping people learn to help themselves and the team.

Change creates Angst and Resistance

You will very probably experience resistance. Some people may be dramatically affected by your style of leadership as contrasted to what they were used to. Keeping alert to concerns throughout your group is very important during the early stages of transition and also something to stay open to throughout your tenure. Paying attention to individuals who are upset and/or are resisting changes is the best tool you have for dealing with these types of concerns. They will appreciate the added attention and it will give you the opportunity to know more about what is driving their concerns. Then you will have a better chance of finding ways to deal with those problems directly.

Call the Kettle Black

I am all for bringing things out in the open and dealing with them head on. If you have a disgruntled employee or a team member who is creating concerns or just not producing, get them in and talk. Backstabbers, negativists, complainers, blamers, etc. can quickly undermine a transition process and the overall atmosphere of the team. Let them know you know there are concerns, get them talking openly about them, get them focused on solutions. Stay on top of what is happening until they begin to take positive responsibility for who they are and what they are doing.

Get help

There are times when an employee or a situation can get out of hand. Use all the resources you have at your disposal. Many businesses have departments that provide assistance in a variety of ways (Human Resources, Legal, Counseling and Coaching, etc.).

> I once had to deal with an alcoholic team member within a few weeks of being on the job. I gathered information, got the employee in and met with him several times (getting things out in the open), talked with my boss and a department that worked with these types of concerns, and in short, dealt with it.

Get information, help, and support when you need it!

Often as managers we have some time to spend with concerns, but we also have a great many obligations. Give the time you can to a person, because that is one of the most important things you can do, but if you have the option, and an employee has a history of being a problem, getting them extra help may be warranted. [Some coaches are trained in working with difficult employees and employee concerns. Other issues may warrant counseling or other support services.]

The earlier in the process of transition that you tackle the 'difficult problems,' the easier they will be to deal with. Leaving personnel concerns on the back burner is asking for more serious concerns down the road.

Take your time, but get people rolling

It is almost inevitable that a new leader is going to make changes. Keeping the focus on the key elements of why change is necessary is important to getting everyone on board, but it is also judicious to change things incrementally, if at all feasible. Design change so that people can succeed and so that they can build from one success to another over time. It probably feels like you want to charge ahead and instigate a dozen things to make everything better all at once, but that is not how your team members will probably see it. Get them moving and then give them the opportunity to assimilate changes so they don't feel overwhelmed. Be sure you keep them moving along, too.

Get things down on paper

I like to get things down on paper or disk: plans, goals, strategies, ideas, the values and qualities you live by and you feel are important to your job and your team's jobs, changes you are instigating, who is involved, etc. It ensures that what is important has not only been said, but it can be referred back to if necessary. It is another one of those ways leaders keep people on their toes. You are bound to have someone on your team who likes to keep everything orderly. Give them the task of taking notes at meetings and compiling important information.

Things You May Have to Deal With

Resistance from your Boss

It is not only possible, but likely, even if he/she hired you to shake things up. Everyone is affected by change and we all have our comfort zones. Be judicious, but move ahead. It pays to find the best way to broach things up the chain. You can also use this technique:

> "Something you said really inspired me to make these changes....," i.e. find a way to give them part of the credit or empower them to be part of the changes.

Resistance from Employees

Some will resist more than others and sometimes the resistance may be very subtle. As discussed above, the more open and forthright you are, and can get them to be, the better. Find ways to pay a bit more attention to the 'trouble makers.'

Complacency

It may be 'how things have been' or it may be that people just don't care any more. Talk about what you stand for and lead the battle line forward into the fray. There are always good to great people on every team who may have fallen into a rut. Get them going and acknowledge, recognize, and award the behaviors you want to see. Once the ball is rolling people will get the message that complacency just isn't part of an accepted approach around here anymore.

The really 'difficult' employees

Unfortunately there usually is one in every bunch (or several). You have to find out enough about them to understand where they are coming from, what they value and find important, and what motivates them. Don't be afraid to ask. Simply paying more positive attention to them may make a big difference. Set up win-win situations for them until they get rolling on their own.

Many (in my experience, most) difficult employees are very talented, they have just gotten off track over the years and need some direction and motivation. If you are the leader of a large team, train some of your subordinates in these types of techniques as well. You can also hire a coach who works specifically with difficult people concerns. (See the Business coaching section at http://www.difficultpeople.org)

Slow downs

We all agree to the changes, we are all motivated to get moving, we charge out of the gate and... something happens along the way.

Changes take a long time to become established. The change process is long and drawn out by anyone's standards. You, as leader, need to bring the significance of what you are striving for back into everyone's purview at every opportunity and you need to make sure you keep your eye on the ball, too. What you do, what you spend time on, what you talk about, what you acknowledge and reward are what your team members will spend their time and focus on, too.

Support the Good Stuff

When we take over a team we tend to be a bit nervous. We are excited, enervated, and motivated to do our best. We exude that in our approach to everything and it shows because we are acknowledging people, helping them understand who we are and what we are all about, and we even reward them fairly regularly with smiles, thanks, and other forms of recognition and reward.

Two weeks later – we are busy being a manager.

Keep up the good stuff. Though the initial energy may have dissipated somewhat, we can still pay attention to and recognize everyone's effort and contributions. In the simplest terms – LEAD!

Questions and Ideas for Contemplation

The better you know your people, the better your life as a manager and leader will be. People will notice and appreciate your efforts to understand who they are and what goes on in the trenches. You will have far fewer difficulties when you are willing to make this effort.

Chapter 23

Dealing with Major Corporate Change

An Acquisition

Major corporate change has become commonplace in our global economy. Companies merge, are bought and sold, Presidents, CEOs, and Chairmen seem to come and go, with restructurings frequently part of their tenure. In this chapter we will explore the impact of change related to a takeover. It is important to keep in mind that the employees of both companies in a merger or takeover are affected by the changes that are the result of the consolidation of the two businesses. Mid-level managers of both companies share the weight of the impact and the responsibility for helping their team members through the long transition process.

Ouch!

Even the announcement of a planned takeover hits people very hard. Initially the employees of the company being acquired will be affected most and the impact will immediately create a great deal of stress. Eventually, as the long range effects of the acquisition are realized, everyone throughout both companies will be affected and will need to make adjustments.

Shock and Confusion

Just knowing that their company is being taken over will have a marked impact on the employees. Shock and disbelief are very common reactions that will quickly be followed by the confusion and concern for what will actually happen to everyone. Unfortunately in spite of the best efforts of the companies and their senior management, typically real information is scanty, and even when the upper administrative levels are open and forthright about what is happening, major corporate change takes time. From the time of the initial announcement, it could take a year or more for the takeover to be completed and for people to know what will happen to them. Then you still have many more months of dealing with the change process as people are assimilated into the 'new' structure and/or become acclimated to the changes taking place.

Manager's Responsibilities

This is one of the hardest times for a mid-level manager. Not only does he/she need to help team members with all the difficulties related to their reactions and concerns about the coming change, he/she has to keep the regular 'business at hand' moving along.

This is where true leadership shows through.

> There is no doubt that mid-level managers are pretty much in the same boat as their team members. They are as likely to lose their jobs, be relocated, or have significant change made to their positions as any employee might. They will probably not have much more information than anyone else in the trenches about what is happening or going to happen.

In spite of your own feelings, fears, and concerns, you still have to lead.

Character

This is where true character shines. Managers must rise above their own worries and difficulties and help their team members in every way possible throughout the change process. Even when you may find out that you and many of the people on your team are going to be 'let go' you still have to be the person who rises to the occasion. At least up until the time comes you walk out the door for the last time. This is what character is all about.

Your greatest skill during difficult change is how you approach the change yourself, i.e. what you are showing your team members. If you need help and support, get it, (coach, mentor, etc.) because what you present outwardly to your employees is what will make a huge difference in how they handle change and the difficulties they will face. Your job becomes even more than ever before one of being a port in the midst of the storm for your employees.

Your solidity and calmness will immeasurably help your team players be able to deal with the difficulties they face.

The Impact of Corporate Change

Emotional Impact

Initial emotions: shock, confusion, apprehension, panic, anger, resentment

Ongoing feelings: Fear, resentment, anger, depression, confusion, vulnerability (see Chapter 2)

What you can do

Be there. Be as confident and stalwart as you can. Be open to concerns. Be willing to listen and commiserate. Provide assistance where you can and seek additional assistance wherever and whenever feasible. Keep in mind that emotional reactions to change are ongoing throughout the entire long change process.

Communications Impact

No information; poor or misinformation; the slow evolution of major corporate change with little information available to mid-level management; rumor mills starting and festering, resulting in negative affect and negative undercurrents

What you can do

Keep the lines of communication open. Keep everyone on your team up-to-date on all communications from above; make sure they understand that you are providing them with all the knowledge you have and are allowed to give them; keep rumor-mongering and negativity to a minimum by being honest about everything and by encouraging open communications

Work reactions

Poor motivation; lowered productivity; poor quality, complacency

What you can do

Keep them moving and involved. It may be very difficult to do this depending on what actually is going on, but one of the best things for everyone is to keep doing what you do best. Keep the team motivated and working toward goals. This can help everyone deal with difficulties with more confidence and control throughout the change process, even when things may be winding down and people moving on.

Continued effort may be beneficial in several ways: keeping everyone involved and productive helps maintain direction and motivation; continued quality productivity may help as things come down to 'crunch time,' as your team may be viewed as a valuable commodity; or it may help with future recommendations and employment. Find reasons for everyone to stay involved. The more focus is brought back to personal and team goals the more people will be able to deal with what happens on a more global scale.

The Impact of the Acquisition

Loss of jobs; relocation; change of management; team changes; loss of position

What you can do

Offer and provide as much support as possible. Help employees face tough decisions by gathering as much information as possible, encouraging them to take advantage of all available resources, and helping them get their resumes and personal information together. Even as things are winding down, a good leader can provide a great deal of support and encouragement for team members. Great leaders will be concerned with their team players while they are working at moving ahead themselves. The best leaders I know help their team members after they have moved on by staying in touch and showing their concern with how their transitions are going.

There is much you can do to facilitate people moving on with their work and lives. Most importantly you provide support throughout the transition process regardless of where you will all end up. People appreciate this type of leadership. They will remember your efforts for the rest of their lives.

Sometimes it boils down to the huge difference that simple things make:

> Helping someone pack their boxes while offering them a kind, supportive word as they prepare to leave

A final pat on the back thanking them for everything they have done

A farewell party for your team where everyone shares a bit of why it was so great to be part of this group and also a brief bit about their plans; and so on.

The Acquiring Company

While the initial impact of change may be considerably less to the managers and personnel of the company that is taking over the 'acquisee,' eventually there will also be a marked impact to the parent company.

What can happen

Teams and corporate structure may be reshaped; personnel may be added or moved from/within teams; new leadership infused at many levels; a melding of corporate cultures which can be very difficult for personnel from both companies; etc.

It is rarely business as usual; it is more likely 'how we are going to do business now.'

What you can do

The key for mid-level managers is to stay with the basics: the fundamental values and qualities that are the focal point of their work ethic. Then it is making sure through open and positive contact that everyone 'gets it.' All of the recommendations above, from Chapter 16, and throughout this book are applicable: being supportive; maintaining personal contact with personnel; open communications; etc.

The Best of the Best

It is human nature at its best that results in all of us eventually moving on and making the best of whatever life and work throws at us. We make hard choices and we roll with the punches. As a leader you cannot predict or control very much of what happens but you can make a DIFFERENCE (that is a VERY BIG difference) to your people by honoring who they are. It is that simple (and that hard, too!)

Questions and Ideas for Contemplation

Front-line and middle managers are the people who make the real differences in whether changes instituted from above will happen effectively and efficiently in an organization. While you may want to throw your hands up in the air and shout, "What were they thinking," the onus is on you to step forward and make things happen.

Get as clear a picture as you can

Root yourself in your values

Take care of your people

And you WILL make a BIG difference!

Chapter 24

Customer Focus

The focus of every business is, in the final analysis, preparing and presenting a product or service for a customer base. Whether that base is another industry or an individual consumer out in the 'real world,' leaders need to be concerned with how change not only impacts their team and/or organization, but also the customers they are working for.

Change Impacts Everyone

How you feel, how your team members feel, affects your work. When you are affected, the consumer is affected. It can be a change in productivity, a lapse in quality, or how attitude is affecting consumer comfort and trust.

If you are the head of a team or division that directly impacts your customer base because your employees are regularly in direct contact with customers, it is important to know how the impact of change is affecting your team members and how that is being translated into their work and interactions with customers.

Even if your team is far-removed from the consumer in manufacturing, research, data collection, etc. your employees' attitude will get out there much sooner than you might think and the effects on productivity, quality, and motivation may have long range impact on customer satisfaction as well.

Create "Total Customer Responsiveness"* Now!

A major emphasis (and section) of Thomas Peters' book, ***Thriving on Chaos: Handbook for a Management Revolution,** focuses on business's paying attention to customers. This is an excellent resource for managerial and leadership customer responsiveness information: "Specialize/Create Niches/Differentiate," "Provide Top Quality as Perceived by the Customer," and "Launch a Customer Revolution," and many other excellent topics.

When change hits a team or organization or even when it is a carefully planned restructuring, it WILL impact the customer. As a leader it is important to help everyone on your team maintain, even within the turmoil that may be going on, a focus on being responsive to customers and receptive to their needs.

This helps fulfill some very important needs in working through change:

> Keeping a keen customer focus helps team members keep their stability through the change process. Though everything else around them may seem to be in a state of turmoil, focusing on the customer, whether it is another team that they provide data for or a consumer, gives them something to root their effort toward – something familiar and generally consistent.

> Focusing away from their own concerns can help team members move from negative feelings or a 'woe is me' attitude and resistance to change, to a positive, 'quality-focused,' 'get it done' position.

> Emphasizing quality and productivity during significant change can get teams focused and moving ahead rather than wallowing in the past and resisting the future. It is an emphasis that leaders can use to refocus their group again and again throughout the change process. Providing direction and purpose can help prevent and alleviate many concerns that would be a 'normal' part of long-term, difficult change.

> Returning to a customer focus gives team leaders many opportunities to provide acknowledgment, recognition, and small wins for their team players throughout the change process. It can not only help get the ball rolling, but help keep it rolling when obstacles are encountered.

> Customer focus is a positive way to get around bureaucratic blockages to successful change. People are more likely to pay attention (especially up the chain) when things are presented in a way in which successful change means happier customers, better productivity and potentially more sales.

Emphasize Responsiveness

Teams that are motivated to respond to customer concerns quickly and creatively are stimulated to more action by their success. The focus is taken away from change and the impact of change as it affects everyone toward "How can we help others," "How can we be our best." It helps keep teams moving in a positive direction. It can also provide impetus for higher levels of excellence.

Take Care of Your People, Too

Leaders can emphasize a customer focus during the change process from the get-go, but there needs to be a balance between taking care of your team members' concerns, and getting them on-board focusing outward to the customer. Both are important. If your total emphasis is on the customer, your team players may become even more disgruntled and feel that what is important to them is not being addressed.

Throughout the change process managers need to be aware of the impact that the change is having on their entire sphere of influence: team members, line and matrix teams that your team impacts, auxiliary/support personnel and teams, AND customers.

Questions and Ideas for Contemplation

When faced with changes at work that impact everyone, be sure to remember to ask this question:

> How can you keep your customer focus during change, and how can you keep your customer service representatives on the top of their game?

See our book, "Succeeding with Difficult Customers," for a comprehensive approach to training customer contact personnel. Available at www.difficultpeople.org.

Chapter 25

Taking Care of Your People

"This above all: to thine own self be true,

And it must follow, as the night the day,

Thou canst not then be false to any man."

(William Shakespeare, *Hamlet*, Polonius sending his son Laertes off to school with good advice)

Managers are concerned about how their teams perform. Leaders are concerned about their people.

There is a big difference!

And both are important

Leaders know that if the people they supervise are happy, motivated, and energized they will perform well.

What leadership qualities make the most difference in how people feel, respond, and perform?

More than anything else,

People will respond to you when you are true to yourself,

When you live and support the values and qualities that are most important to you.

NOTE: We have listed 99 values and qualities that we feel are important to leadership in *Honoring Work and Life: 99 Words for Leaders to Live By.* (See Appendix II for a copy of this list and an exercise you can do to prioritize leadership qualities you value.)

Keys to Motivation

True motivation comes from the heart, not from a bombastic, enervating speech (though these have their purpose, too). The keys to keeping people happy with their work, motivated, and energized are (in this particular order!):

Caring – However you are comfortable in showing that your people are important to you as people, not just as tools to get something done.

Attention – Paying attention to people out where they are working shows a desire to understand work from their perspective. Making this effort should be a top priority of every leader and manager. It seems like it should be such a simple thing to do, but it isn't. We have to make the effort every day, because no one likes to feel ignored. Also, keep in mind, the more difficult a person, the more attention they need because of their insecurity. If you pay them more positive attention, you will have fewer concerns with them from the get-go.

Understanding – Stay open to others' take on things. It is one of the best ways to learn, and it matters. Everyone appreciates someone making an effort to understand who they are and what is important to them.

Compassion and Kindness – These go hand and hand with all the terms above and below. There are always ways to say even difficult things in a kind and compassionate way. It is a skill you can learn through observation of how you say things and through practice. It is worth the effort.

Acknowledgment and Appreciation – Again, it is such a simple gift and takes such little effort to do this regularly, but unfortunately we let so many opportunities go by. A thank, you, a pat on the back, a two sentence e-mail, a kind word in passing – every one of these means more than any evaluation system. Period! Every leader needs to remind themselves of this every day.

P.S. Say 'thanks,' frequently.

Recognition, Celebration, Reward, and Ceremony – all great ways to build esprit.

Here is a good hint: often the simplest things work the best. You don't have to spend huge amounts of money or time to recognize people. The little gestures mean a lot.

Staying on Top of Things

Our work and our home lives intermingle a great deal. A quality leader knows when one of his people is hurting and could use some support or assistance. Sometimes it is simply stopping by with a kind word, or a 'I hope things work out for you.' At other times, you may be able to offer support, mentoring, recommendations for assistance, etc. Many large businesses have programs and support services that their employees can take advantage of. Find out what is available in house and in the local area so that you can help point people in the right direction.

There is always a fine line between what is appropriate and what isn't in working with employee concerns. The best way to find out is to ask,

> "What can I do/provide that will help you with this concern?"

Or ask them if they are comfortable with your helping.

> "Francis, I know you are dealing with some personal concerns right now. I just wanted to let you know I am here if you need anything. Is there anything I can do to help right now?"

Being Available

A leader covers a lot of ground by creating an atmosphere that says, "I'm here for you. I'm available if you have concerns. I will do whatever I can for you as an individual and for this team. We are in this together."

Then be sure you live up to this 'unspoken' bargain.

Always try to make time for someone with a concern. You will end up having far fewer concerns in the long run.

Stand up for your folks!

This is one of my pet peeves – bosses who are reluctant to go to bat for their people. I have worked for several. If you can't or won't do something for a team player, then let them know why. If you tried and failed, then let them know the details. Honesty is always the best policy – always!

Being willing to make an effort is what counts. It is one of those characteristics that really separate the great leaders from the not-so-great.

A Final Word (from Shakespeare)

> "Farewell; my blessing season this in thee!"
>
> (End of Polonius' speech)

Questions and Ideas for Contemplation

There are many ways in which you can support, encourage, and take care of your people. Seek them out; implement them. People who you take care of, will invariably find ways to take care of you.

Chapter 26

Taking Care of You

Stress and overwork are the watchwords of today's business executive.

How are you measuring up?

Or down?

I am all for hard work, making something of ourselves, and even keeping up with the Joneses. However, you should be able to enjoy your life AND your work. The following key ideas can help.

The rest IS up to you.

Time Management

Am I repeating myself? Make the choice to make a difference by accepting responsibility for your time concerns. Then make a difference by changing things and sticking to the changes. Remember: the tendency is to just add more work – don't – add some fun, too.

Stress Management

The amazing thing about stress is we live with it day in and day out, we bring it home with us, and we even sleep with it. We have gotten so used to it, we rarely notice it any more unless it reaches a fever pitch or we have our first heart attack. DEAL WITH IT!

There are lots of ideas for stress reduction. Pick from this list or find your own favorites. The important thing is to do something every day, preferably several times a day. It doesn't have to take much time.

TAKE A BREAK!

A short relaxing walk (walking from one meeting to another or talking on your cell phone doesn't count)

A two minute meditative silence (five or ten if you really want to make a difference) – this is amazingly effective.

Meditate – arrange for a short period of time for an undisturbed break (five – twenty minutes or so); meditate on something pleasurable. If you like more structure, take some classes and learn how, but a brief positive relaxation is what you are after.

Take some deep breaths – I like to think of breathing out the bad stuff and breathing in the good. Powerful!

Take a half day off to spend time with someone you care about, and remember to forget about work for those four hours!

Actually take a vacation – You could even try it without your computer and cell phone along. I dare you!

Keep an inspiring book handy and take a few minutes to read a thought several times a day. It is even better if you spend a couple more minutes contemplating the idea(s) you just read.

Do something positive for someone else. It is great for stress and the best feeling there is.

Call someone just because – your significant other, kid, an old friend

Get some exercise – it can help energize you in the middle of the day.

Know your Limits

There are times when we have to take a step back and force ourselves to take a break. It might be just a few moments to regain composure or an actual vacation to just get away. Pushing yourself past what you can comfortably put up with makes for a whole host of problems…

Not the least of which is you are becoming a more difficult person to work and live with.

If you doubt this, be willing to ask someone the next time you are 'stressed out.'

Take Care of...

> The physical You
>
> The intellectual You
>
> The psychological You
>
> The spiritual You

Be able to and willing to say, "NO!"

Hint: It is your choice, not 'theirs'.

Celebrate what is Right with YOUR Life...

...by focusing on the good stuff. The bad stuff will demand enough of your attention as it is. This is a choice we make many times a day. Find ways in which you can enjoy all of the moments you can.

Big Hint: Making someone else's day by paying attention to them and helping take care of them is one of the best ways to celebrate what is right with your life, too.

Finding your WOWS!*

I can name a dozen WOWS in my life without thinking very hard – related to both my work and my life. WOW!

So can you.

Spend a little time each day enjoying the great things about your work and life

and, guess what?

You will spend less time worrying, stressing, judging...

*Tom Peters doesn't own this word, but he loves to write about it. See bibliography.

Smile

And find things every day to smile about. They are there and you don't even have to look hard, but you do have to pay attention.

When you take care of YOU,
you will take care of others, too!

Questions and Ideas for Contemplation

It pays to self-evaluate your 'fun' quotient every day.

"If you are not having fun, something's wrong...

Adjust!"

(Difficultpeople.org)

Make up your own enjoyment scale and keep track for a week or a month. How did you do? Just doing this should help you pay more attention to your stress level.

You could also make up a stress scale and see how that pans out after a month, but you would be focusing on the wrong thing.

Chapter 27

Winning Small/Winning Big

Winning Small

This means paying attention to and making the most of all the small wins you have at work day in and day out.

It supports others

Helps everyone feel better

Makes a huge difference in morale and cohesiveness

Keeps everyone moving ahead.

It doesn't take a lot of time

It costs relatively nothing

It can happen spontaneously when something goes right – which is often the best kind of small win.

Helping people to win small during times of difficult change is particularly important. Though the future may be uncertain and everyone is stressed, worried, and off-balance, little wins can help keep them moving positively and in the right direction.

Small wins serve as guideposts through to the next big hurdle.

Use your insight as a leader to pick the right moments and efforts to highlight. Spread the wealth around, but be sure to be sincere and fair. Remember that a quick smile or a 'thanks' at just the right moment can send just as big a message as a bouquet of flowers or a letter of commendation.

Get out and about to really make a difference with this. Impromptu and spontaneous acts of gratitude and praise mean wonders to stressed and worried personnel. Help people to win; it helps create many more wins down the road.

Winning Big

Winning those big ones often comes from all those little wins that gave your people the impetus and commitment to get to this point.

Winning big is about appreciation, recognition, celebration, and ceremony. It is making a big 'to do' about accomplishments of your team and of individuals on your team.

Celebrate what is right with your team by making sure those big wins get recognized at every level. Let your people know that what they have done is not just about this team at this place in time, but that it is something that means something to the whole organization, the vision, and the mission. Make sure that your team members know that you have broadcast their accomplishments up, down, and through the chain of command. When you make that kind of effort, it will make a difference to how they feel about themselves and each other...and you, too.

Questions and Ideas for Contemplation

List the small wins you have made something of the past month. Resolve to double or triple that figure in the next WEEK! See what happens.

Take the next big win opportunity and see what special way you can commemorate the accomplishment. Get creative. Ask your team members for ideas. Have some fun with it.

Chapter 28

Staying in Touch

This is one of the most important ideas in this book and it has two distinct emphases:

> Staying in touch with yourself
>
> Staying in touch with others

Staying in touch with yourself: Key ideas

Great leaders know themselves. The have a good handle on who they are, what they value, how they present themselves to the world, and how what they do impacts others. During times of change when concerns and difficulties seem to pile on top of each other for your attention, being in-control and having a solid sense of self makes all the difference in how you lead.

Developing and maintaining a solid sense of self-worth is accomplished by the hard work of paying attention to all the things listed below. It takes time, but it is worth the effort.

Know yourself

> The values and qualities you aspire to and admire in others
>
> Your communications and how they impact others
>
> What you spend time on
>
> How you feel – How that impacts others.
>
> What you think – How that impacts others.
>
> Your reactions and responses to others:

Remember

Positivity – How you feel rubs off

Negativity – Worrying, Blaming, Complaining, Judging, Defensiveness (all signs of Ego and a poor sense of self-worth)- unfortunately, also rubs off on others.

Take care of yourself

> Time and Stress management
>
> Physically
>
> Emotionally
>
> Psychologically
>
> Spiritually

Staying in touch with others

The best leaders I know pay attention to others. They do it by getting out in the trenches and being with them; they do it by supporting them. For me, this isn't a "Well, if I have time," item, this is at the top of the charts of wise, quality leadership. It is a responsibility. It should be something that happens daily.

Show them

That you care – that they are more than a cog in the wheel of the business machine. However you are comfortable with showing humanity to others, make the effort through,

> Attention
>
> Acknowledgment
>
> Appreciation – learn to say 'Thanks' a lot
>
> Recognition
>
> Support – a willingness to go to bat for them, especially in difficult circumstances where your mettle needs to show, and their mettle will more likely show as a result of what you do
>
> Understanding
>
> Encouragement
>
> Respect
>
> Courteousness

Leadership in Times of Change...

is all about people and how you work with them.

It is all about people and how you work for them.

You can formulate wonderful plans, detail strategies, and aim for terrific goals, but the real grass roots is about what you do and how that affects your team members, your coworkers, and all the other people who impact your work life.

You are in Charge Now

And you can do as you damned well please. However, you might want to consider keeping this phrase in the back of your mind:

Choose Wisely

Wishing you the best, and a successful career as a caring leader,

Joe Koob

Appendix I

The Seven Keys to Being Successful with Difficult People

These seven key ideas are the backbone of the materials presented throughout the Difficultpeople.org website. They have been developed by Dr. Koob through his extensive experience and study relevant to difficult people and difficult situations. As you begin to understand more and more about dealing successfully with difficult people come back to these Key Ideas. You will find they offer a tremendous amount of insight and support.

The "Seven Keys to being Successful with Difficult People" came about through the ongoing development of literature available at www.difficultpeople.org – a web site dedicated to "Understanding and Working with Difficult People." As you work on your understanding and strengths in these important areas you will notice a marked difference and improvement in how you perceive 'difficult' people you interact with and how you handle their 'difficult' interpersonal behaviors.

These "Seven Keys" are all centered in your attitude about yourself and others

Working successfully with other people centers around how we feel about ourselves. Their 'stuff' has a direct effect on <u>how they interact with us</u> but does not have to affect how we feel or go about our own work. When we can step beyond their problems and live our life to the fullest and make the most of our work on OUR terms, we have learned to truly be in control.

Self-awareness

Self-worth

Self-Confidence

Self-Control

Honesty

Kindness

Positivity

Self-awareness

Self-awareness tops this list because it is fundamental to all the other ideas. When we begin to understand ourselves better, we can make better choices, and we strengthen our self-worth, self-confidence, and self-control. There is no better tool available for you to help build your foundation for dealing effectively and positively with others.

Working on your self-awareness pays big dividends. It is helpful to start this process by reading more extensive materials on how to develop these skills. [See *Understanding and Working with Difficult People*; *Me! A Difficult Person?* and *A Perfect Day: Guide for a Better Life (Koob, J.)*]

Self-worth

Self-worth is how we value ourselves. It has nothing to do with ego – placing ourselves above others. It has to do with who we truly believe ourselves to be and how we bring that belief to the world. It has to do with understanding our most fundamental values – who we would most like to be with others.

Self-confidence

As we develop our self-worth our self-confidence improves. Many of the difficulties we have with other people are affected a great deal by our inability to maintain a confident and positive demeanor when we are with them. You can be assured that if you are getting upset, defensive, depressed, etc. that your confidence is taking a hit.

Self-confident people approach others from an assertive stance. Assertiveness is being able to accept yourself in an interaction with another person regardless of their behavior. It does take practice and self-awareness.

Self-control

Control of other people is an illusion. It is an illusion that drives difficult people to their difficult behaviors. To be successful with difficult people our only recourse is **self-control**. We are not out to control them, only our own feelings, thoughts, and responses to their difficult behaviors. When we are in control, they almost always don't have any choice but to change their negative behavior when interacting with us.

No one can control our lives without our permission! We always have positive choices we can make. Sometimes they are difficult to understand or to see. Practice in self-awareness, awareness and understanding of others, and in developing our self-worth and self-confidence can make all the difference.

Honesty

Honesty means being honest with ourselves (more self-awareness!) and being **kindly** honest with others.

You always have a right to be honest with others and there are ALWAYS positive, assertive ways to do that.

Kindness

Every interaction we have with other people has the opportunity for us to be kind, or to be something else. Practicing kindness, especially in the face of difficult behavior, pays huge dividends. Try it! You will be pleasantly surprised.

It can be really tough to be kind and compassionate in the face of a very disagreeable, inflexible person. Try to keep in mind that this difficult person is a child of the universe no less than you. Whatever 'stuff,' past and current, has them where they currently are, is perhaps quite unfortunate, for you, and especially for them. You may be able to make a positive difference to their existence, even if it is only for a short time. And you may very well be the catalyst that helps them start to turn their life around.

Positivity

This can be summed up in one of Dr. Koob's favorite sayings:

Negativity breeds Negativity

Positivity Breeds Positivity

Choose Wisely

Another way to say this is:

Negativity NEVER helps!

These are well worth thinking about as often as possible!

Appendix II

99 Words for Leaders to Live By

INTEGRITY

1. Integrity
2. Honesty**
3. Trust
4. Ownership
5. Accountable
6. Responsibility
7. Reliability
8. Self-control**
9. Loyalty
10. Committed
11. Conscientious
12. Credible
13. Stability
14. Continuity
15. Disciplined
16. Humility
17. Idealism

SERVICE to Others

18. Service
19. Appreciation
20. Acknowledgment
21. Respect
22. Courteous
23. Attention
24. Support
25. Grateful (Thanking People)
26. Recognition
27. Celebration
28. Ceremony
29. Reward

HONORING the Humanity of Others

30. Caring
31. Kindness**
32. Empathy
33. Compassion
34. Patience
35. Generous
36. Responsiveness
37. Grace

PERCEPTION

38. Self-awareness**
39. Awareness
40. Visibility
41. Connecting
42. Modeling

SELF-VALUE

43. Self-worth**
44. Self-respect
45. Self-confidence**
46. Character
47. Identity

QUALITY

48. Quality
49. Value-added
50. Stretching
51. Learning
52. Education
53. Renewal
54. Solution-focused
55. Catalyst
56. Cultivate
57. Rigorous

PERSONAL APPROACH

58. Persistence
59. Synthesizer
60. Cohesion
61. Attitude
62. Consistent
63. Cooperative
64. Competent
65. Discerning
66. Focus
67. Organized
68. Engagement
69. Determined
70. Energy
71. Down-to-earth
72. Simplicity

FREE YOURSELF

73. Creativity
74. Innovation
75. Flexibility
76. Experiment
77. Risk-taking
78. Fluidity
79. Chances
80. Imagination
81. Friction-free
82. Anticipates

83. Facilitates

84. Curiosity

85. Initiative

86. Choices

LIVE LIFE OUT LOUD

87. Passion

88. Vision

89. Conviction

90. Courage

91. Fearless

92. Zany

93. Spontaneous

94. Zesty

95. Intensity

96. Charisma

97. Showmanship

98. Positivity**

99. Symbolizes

Exercise

Select the ten most relevant words to your perspective of leadership – what qualities and values do you most admire and strive to emulate?

If possible, select the top five, top three, and the most important quality to you from this short list.

You may use other terms/phrases. Come up with the list that best describes who you are and what you value as a leader and person. These qualities and values will help you set the stage for your developing into the best leader possible.

[This list of 99 leadership values and qualities comes from *Honoring Work and Life: 99 Words for Leaders to Live By*, by Dr. Joseph Koob]

Appendix III

Annotated Bibliography of Difficultpeople.org Materials

Understanding and Working with Difficult People

We believe this book presents the most comprehensive material available about being successful with difficult people. This book is designed to be a practical, accessible introduction to the very broad topic of dealing with difficult people/difficult behaviors. Since every difficult situation is different, the focus here will be on building a basic understanding of how you interact with difficult people, what makes difficult people tick, and the most fundamental skills you can bring to the table to help change these encounters for the better.

ME! A Difficult Person?

This is second of our signature books. This book focuses on learning more about yourself. Most of us are occasionally difficult or seen as difficult by others. This may simply be a matter of different perspectives, or it may mean that we have some inner work to do. This course is concerned with understanding more about how you come across to others, and understanding more about who you are as a person. It is also concerned with self-improvement – making changes that will help make your interactions with others significantly better, and that will bring you more peace, comfort, and joy in your life.

Difficult Spouses? Improving and Saving Your Relationship with Your Significant Other

Are you having difficulties in your current relationship? Facing a divorce? Newly divorced and trying to understand what happened and what you could have done about it? We feel this book has value not only for couples who are simply having difficulties in their relationships with their significant others; those facing divorce, recently divorced couples; and for people entering new relationships. The focus is on developing the knowledge, skills, and tools to help your relationship be successful.

Dealing with Difficult Strangers

Being successful in difficult situations with strangers is all about what you can bring to the situation. You will find a tremendous amount of useful information and skills included in this book that can make a significant difference in how you approach difficult strangers, how you feel as a result of these difficult encounters, and how you can emerge without a negative experience having ruined your day.

Succeeding with Difficult Professors (and Tough Courses)

A course for college students at all levels. What you need to know to make the most of your college career. This course has two main sections: "Getting along with Difficult Professors," and "Succeeding in Tough Classes." The first section will discuss ideas and skills you can use to get through personal difficulties with professors. The second section will focus on techniques, study skills, and approaches that will help you get the grades you want.

Guiding Children

Guiding and working with children is on the mind of every parent. This book focuses on skills and tools to help you as a parent provide the best possible environment for your child's development by avoiding difficulties through intelligent upbringing. This book is not only about helping you to guide your children through concerns that arise, but it is even more about enjoying your children. They do grow up, much faster than we expect. Take advantage of the tremendous joy they can bring into your life and the vast understanding of life that they provide. You will be glad you did.

Business Trilogy: Dealing with Change

Difficult Situations - Dealing with Change

Difficult situations can certainly produce a great deal of angst and as a result, difficult people. From my own long personal experience, I know that when things are tough, I can get much more difficult than normal. Those are the times when I know I need to deal with my own stuff.

Honoring Work and Life: 99 Words for Leaders to Live By

This book provides a foundation of key ideas that focus on Leadership (and Personal) qualities, attributes, and behaviors that honor not only our work but our life. It is my firm belief that true leaders work to serve their fellow employees, their team, their company, their customers, as well as their families and friends. This is about understanding and working on those attributes that make great leaders.

Leaders Managing Change

Leaders Managing Change is about understanding and dealing with the ongoing stresses of constant change in the business world today, but most importantly it is about leadership. When I thought about the concerns that are a regular part of high turnover rates, leadership changes, acquisitions and mergers, and the myriad of other transitions businesses face today, the focus came down to leadership. Good leaders get things done. This book focuses on knowledgeable leadership, i.e. what you need to know to help you deal with change as a leader. It presumes you are already inspired, good, intelligent, and practical. This book is about making a difference.

Dealing with Difficult Customers

(for Employees, Companies, and Customer Service Personnel)

This book is all about putting the gamut of customer relations and interactions into a perspective that is workable, livable, and supports you, the customer contact person, throughout.

While many businesses do provide extensive customer relations training, the focus is often fairly one way – aimed at keeping business. We present you with extensive insight and knowledge about the customer's perspective, what you need to know as a company representative to fulfill your job, the internal and external support you need, and the tools and skills to communicate effectively with difficult customers.

Business Trilogy: Succeeding at Work

Dealing with Difficult Coworkers

This work is one that based on my research is a needed addition to the difficult people literature. There are a number of books available that discuss difficult people in the workplace, but do not focus specifically on coworkers. There are different dynamics between bosses and employees, employees and their peers, and employees with their bosses. The emphasis here is on helping people solve the difficulties they have at work with someone who is relatively speaking a 'coworker,' or 'colleague,' in other words, someone whose 'rank' or 'job' is roughly on the same level as theirs.

Succeeding with Difficult Bosses

Have a tough boss? This is a practical, in-the-trenches approach to succeeding with a difficult authority figure – a (how to) book for one of your most important relationships at work.

Managing Difficult Employees

In Production

Caring for Difficult Patients: A Guide for Nursing Professionals

I believe that the Nursing profession is one of the most admired in America. We think of Nurses as professional: that is, they have a knowledge base and skill set that is unique and valued – the quality of their work is important to them; and we think of Nurses as people who care about their patients – they are concerned with our well-being when we are under their care. These considerations are the focal point for discussing how to best deal with difficult patients.

Bibliography

Books and other works on Change and Leadership

Bolles, Richard N., *What Color is Your Parachute?* Ten Speed Press, Berkeley, CA, 1987.

Bridges, William, *Managing Transitions: Making the Most of Change*, Perseus Books, Cambridge, 1991.

Bridges, William, *Transitions: Making Sense of Life's Changes*, Perseus Books, Cambridge, 1980.

Buckingham, Marcus, & Coffman, Curt, *First, Break All the Rules: What the World's Greatest Managers Do Differently*, Simon and Schuster, New York, 1999.

Collins, J., and Porras, J., *Built to Last: Successful Habits of Visionary Companies*, Harper Business, NY, 2001.

Collins, Jim, *Good TO Great: Why Some Companies Make the Leap...and Others Don't*, Harper Business, NY, 2001.

Cooper, Robert and Sawaf, Ayman, *Executive EQ: Emotional Intelligence in Leadership & Organizations*, Grisset/Putnam, New York, 1996.

Crane, Thomas, *The Heart of Coaching*, FTA Press, San Diego, 1998.

Deits, Bob, Life *After Loss: A Personal Guide Dealing with Death, Divorce, Job Change and Relocation*, Fisher Books, Tucson, 1988.

Dominhguez, Linda R., *How to Shine at Work*, McGraw Hill, 2003.

Drucker, Peter F., *Managing in a Time of Great Change*, Truman Talley Books, NY, 1995.

Evard, Beth L. And Gipple, Craig A., *Managing Business Change for Dummies*, Hungry Minds, Inc., NY, 2001.

Farson, Richard and Keyes, Ralph, *Whoever Makes the Most Mistakes Wins: The Paradox of Innovation*, Free Press, NY, 2002.

Fortgang, Laura Berman, *Take Yourself to the Top: The Secrets of America's #1 Career Coach*, Warner Books, New York, 1998.

Gates, Bill, *Business @ the Speed of Thought: Succeeding in the Digital Economy*, Warner Books, New York, 1999.

Gerstner, Jr., Louis, V, *Who Says Elephants Can't Dance? Leading a Great Enterprise Through Dramatic Change*, HarperBusiness, New York, 2002.

Going Through Bereavement–When a loved one dies, Langeland Memorial Chapel, Kalamazoo, MI.

Grieve, Bradly T., *The Blue Day Book: A Lesson in Cheering Yourself Up*, Andrews McMeel Publishing, Kansas City, 2000.

Goldratt, Eliyahu M., *Critical Chain*, North River Press, Great Barrington, MA, 1997.

Hammer, Michael and Champy, James, *Reengineering the Corporation: A Manifesto for Business Revolution, HarperBusiness*, New York, 1993.

Hoffer, Eric, *The Ordeal of Change*, Harper & Row, NY, 1952.

Jeffreys, J. Shep. *Coping with Workplace Change: Dealing with Loss and Grief*, Crisp Productions, Menlo Park, CA, 1995.

Johnson, Spencer, *Who Moved My Cheese*, G. P. Putnam, New York, 1998.

Kanter, Rosabeth Moss, *The Change Masters: Innovation & Entrepreneurship in the American Corporation*, Simon & Schuster, New York, 1983.

Kelley, Robert, *How to be a Star at Work: Nine Breakthrough Strategies You Need to Succeed*, Random House, New York, 1998.

Koob, Joseph E. II, *Difficult Situations: Dealing with Change*, NEJS Publications, Saline, MI, 2004.

Kotter, John P, *Leading Change*, Harvard Business School Press, Boston, 1996.

Kotter, John P, *The Leadership Factor*, Free Press, New York, 1988.

Kouzes, J. and Posner, B., *Credibility: How Leaders Gain and Lose it; Why People Demand it*, Jossey-Bass Publishers, San Francisco, 1993.

Kuster, Elizabeth, *Exorcising Your Ex*, Fireside, New York, 1996.

Leonard, George, *Mastery: The Keys to Success and Long-term Fulfillment*, Plume, NY 1992.

Lunden, Joan, and Cagan, Andrea, *A Bend in the Road is Not the End of the Road*, William Morrow, New York, 1998.

Maxwell, John C., *The 21 Indispensible Qualities of Leadership: Becoming the Person Others Will Want to Follow*, Thomas Nelson Publishers, Nashville, 1999.

Maxwell, John C., *The 17 Indisputable Laws of Teamwork: Embrace them and Empower Your Team*, Thomas Nelson Publishers, Nashville, 2001.

Maxwell, John C., *21 Irrefutable Laws of Leadership*, Thomas Nelson, Inc., Nashville, 1998.

Milwid, Beth, *Working With Men: Professional Women Talk About Power, Sexuality, and Ethics*, Beyond Words, Kingsport, TN, 1990.

McKay, Harvey, *Swim with the Sharks: Without Being Eaten Alive*, William Morrow Co., New York, 1988.

Messer, Bonnie J., *Dealing with Change*, Abington Press, 1996.

Montalbo, Thomas, *The Power of Eloquence: Magic Key to Success in Public Speaking*, Prentive-Hall, Englewood Cliffs, N.J., 1984.

Pasternack, Bruce and Viscio, Albert, *The Centerless Corporation: A New Model for Transforming Your Organization for Growth and Prosperity*, Fireside, New York, 1998.

Peters, Tom, *The Circle of Innovation: You Can't Shrink Your Way to Greatnness*, Vintage Books, New York, 1999.

Peters, Tom, *Liberation Management: Necessary Disorganization for the Nanosecond Nineties*, Faucett Columbine, New York, 1992.

Peters, Tom, and Waterman, Robert, *In Search of Excellence: Lessons from America's Best-Run Companies*, Harper & Row, New York, 1982.

Peters, Tom, and Austin, Nancy, *A Passion for Excellence: The Leadership Difference*, Random House, New York, 1985.

Peters, Tom, *The Pursuit of WOW! Every Person's Guide to Topsy-Turvy Times*, Vintage Books, New York, 1994.

Peters, Tom, *Professional Service Firm 50: Fifty Ways to Transform Your "Department" into a Professional Service Firm whose Trademarks are Passion and Excellence*, Alfred A. Knopf, 1999.

Peters, Tom, *Re-imagine! Business Excellence in a Disruptive Age*, DK, London, 2003.

Peters, Tom, *Thriving on Chaos: Handbook for a Management Revolution*, Alfred Knopf, New York, 1987

Popcorn, Faith, *EVEolutuon: The Eight Truths of Marketing to Women*, Hyperion Books, 2001.

Smith, Hyrum W. The *10 Natural Laws of Successful Time and Life Management: Proven Strategies for Increased Productivity and Inner Peace*, Warner Books, New York, 1994.

Talbot, Kay, *The Ten Biggest Myths About Grief*, Abbey Press, St. Meinrad, IN, 2000.

Waterman, Robert H., Jr., *The Renewal Factor: How The Best Get And Keep The Competitive Edge*, Bantam, New York, 1986.

Whitmore, John, *Coaching for Performance*, Nicholas Brealey Publishing, London, 1999.

Difficult People Materials

Axelrod, A and Holtje, J., *201 Ways to Deal with Difficult People*, McGraw-Hill, New York, 1997.

Bell, A. and Smith, D., *Winning with Difficult People*, Barron's, New York, 1997

Bramson, Robert M., *Coping with Difficult Bosses*, Fireside, New York, 1992.

Bramson, Robert M., *Coping with Difficult People*, Anchor Press, New York, 1981.

Braunstein, Barbara, *How to Deal with Difficult People*, Skillpath Publications, Mission, KS, 1994. [Tapes]

Brinkman, R. and Kirschner, R., *Dealing with People You Can't Stand,* McGraw-Hill, New York, 1994.

Carter, Jay, *Nasty Bosses: How to STOP BEING HURT by them without stooping to THEIR level*, McGraw-Hill, New York, 2004.

Case, Gary and Rhoades-Baum, *How to Handle Difficult Customers*, Help Deck Institute, Colorado Springs, 1994.

Cava, Roberta, *Dealing with Difficult People: How to Deal with Nasty Customers, Demanding Bosses and Annoying Co-workers*, Firefly Books, Buffalo, NY, 2004.

Cava, Roberta, *difficult people: How to Deal with Impossible clients, Bosses, and Employees*, Firefly Books, Buffalo, NY, 1990.

Cavaiola, A. And Lavender, N., *Toxic Coworkers: How to Deal with Dysfunctional People on the Job*, New Harbinger Publications, Oakland, CA, 2000.

Costello, Andrew, *How to Deal with Difficult People*, Ligori Publications, Liguri, MI, 1980.

Crowe, Sandra, *Since Strangling Isn't An Option*, Perigee, New York, 1999.

Diehm, William, *How to Get Along with Difficult People*, Broadman Press, Nashville, 1992.

Felder, Leonard, *Does Someone Treat You Badly? How to Handle Brutal Bosses, Crazy Coworkers...and Anyone Else Who Drives You Nuts*, Berkley Books, NY, 1993.

First, Michael, Ed., *Diagnostic and Statistical Manual for Mental Disorders*, 4th Edition, American Psychiatric Asso.,Washington, 1994.

Friedman, Paul, *How to Deal with Difficult People*, SkillPath Publications, Mission, KS, 1994.

Gill, Lucy, *How to Work with Just About Anyone*, Fireside, New York, 1999.

Griswold, Bob, *Coping with Difficult and Negative People and Personal Magnetism*, Effective Learning Systems, Inc., Edina, MN. [Tape]

Holloway, Andy, "Bad Boss Blues," *Canadian Business*, 24 Oct 2004.

Hoover, John, *How to Work for an Idiot: Survive & Thrive Without Killing Your Boss*, Career Press, Princeton, NJ, 2004.

Jones, Katina, *Succeeding with Difficult People*, Longmeadow Press, Stamford, CT, 1992.

Keating, Charles, *Dealing with Difficult People*, Paulist Press, New York, 1984.

Littauer, Florence, *How to Get Along with Difficult People*, Harvest House, Eugene, 1984.

Lloyd, Ken, *Jerks at Work: How to Deal with People Problems and Problem People*, Career Press, Franklin Lakes, NJ, 1999

Lundin, W. and Lundin, J., *When Smart People Work for Dumb Bosses: How to Survive in a Crazy and Dysfunctional Workplace*, McGraw-Hill, New York, 1998.

Markham, Ursula, *How to deal with Difficult people*, Thorsons, London, 1993.

Meier, Paul, *Don't Let Jerks Get the Best of You: Advice for Dealing with Difficult People*, Thomas Nelson, Nashville, 1993.

Namie, G. and Namie, R., *the Bully at Work*, Sourcebooks, Inc., Naperville, IL, 2000.

Osbourne, Christina, *Dealing with Difficult People*, DK, London, 2002.

Oxman, Murray, *The How to Easily Handle Difficult People, Success Without Stress*, Morro Bay, CA, 1997.

Perkins, Betty, *Lion Taming: The Courage to Deal with Difficult People Including Yourself*, Tzedakah Publications, Scramento, 1995.

Rosen, Mark, *Thank You for Being Such A Pain: Spiritual Guidance for Dealing with Difficult People*, Three Rivers Press, New York, 1998.

Segal, Judith, *Getting Them to See It Your Way: Dealing with Difficult and Challenging People*, Lowell House, Los Angeles, 2000.

Solomon, Muriel, *Working with Difficult People*, Prentice Hall, Englewood Cliffs,1990.

Toropov, Brandon, *The Complete Idiot's Guide to Getting Along with Difficult People*, Alpha Books, New York, 1997.

Toropov, Brandon, *Manager's Guide to Dealing with Difficult People*, Prentice Hall, Paramus, NJ, 1997.

Turecki, Stanley, *The Difficult Child*, Bantam Books, NY, 1989.

Weiner, David L., *Power Freaks: Dealing with Them in the Workplace or Anywhere*, Prometheus Books, Amherst, New York, 2002

Weiss, Donald, *How to Deal with Difficult People*, Amacon, New York, 1987.

Recommended Readings

Dewey, John, *Democracy and Education*, Norwood Press, Norwood, MA, 1916.

Dewey, John, *Education and Experience*, Kappa Delta Pi Publications, Macmillian, New York, 1938.

Dyer, Wayne, *Pulling Your Own Strings*, Funk and Wagnalls, New York, 1978.

Dyer, Wayne, *Your Erroneous Zones*, Funk and Wagnalls, New York, 1976.

Dyer, Wayne, *Your Sacred Self*, Harper, New York, 1995.

Guraik, David B., Editor, *Webster's New World Dictionary*, World Publishing, New York, 1972.

Heinlein, Robert, *Time Enough for Love*, New English Library, New York, 1974.

Hesse, Hermann, *Narcissus and Goldmund*, Bantam, New York, 1971.

James, M, and Jongeward, D. *Born to Win*, Addison-Wesley, 1971.

Koob, Joseph, *A Perfect Day: Guide for A Better Life*, NEJS Publications, Lawton, OK, 1998.

Parrott, Thomas Marc, Ed., *Shakespeare: Twenty-three Plays and the Sonnets*, Charles Scribner's Sons, Washington, D.C., 1938.

Pirsig, Robert, *Zen and the Art of Motorcycle Maintenance*, Bantam, New York, 1980.

Rand, Ayn, *Atlas Shrugged*, Signet Books, New York, 1957.

Redman, Ben Ray, Editor, *The Portable Voltaire*, Viking Press, New York, 1949.